Robert C. Metcalf

Language Exercises

Robert C. Metcalf

Language Exercises

ISBN/EAN: 9783337119546

Printed in Europe, USA, Canada, Australia, Japan

Cover: Foto ©ninafisch / pixelio.de

More available books at **www.hansebooks.com**

METCALF'S LANGUAGE SERIES

LANGUAGE EXERCISES

BY

ROBERT C. METCALF

SUPERVISOR OF SCHOOLS, BOSTON, MASS.

AND

ORVILLE T. BRIGHT

SUPERINTENDENT OF SCHOOLS, ENGLEWOOD, ILL.

IVISON, BLAKEMAN, AND COMPANY
Publishers
NEW YORK AND CHICAGO

PREFACE.

THE *use* of language is controlled very largely by *habit.* Hence, language *teaching* resolves itself into such training as will tend to form correct habits of speaking and writing.

Technical grammar is the science of language. We study it to learn of the construction of sentences and of the forms and uses of words. Such knowledge will doubtless help us to a *critical* rather than to the *ordinary* use of language. He who depends upon his knowledge of Grammar to help him through a speech, or even in his every-day conversation, will doubtless find that his thoughts, when they are seeking expression in words, are far from Grammars and grammatical rules. He will find that the fluency and correctness of his speech depend almost entirely upon habits which have been formed by long practice.

Professor W. D. Whitney, in the preface to his *Essentials of English Grammar*, very truly says:—

"It is constant use and practice, under never-failing watch and correction, that makes good writers and speakers; the application of direct authority is the most efficient corrective. Grammar has its part to contribute, but rather in the higher than the lower stages of the work. One must be a somewhat reflective user of language to amend even here and there a point by grammatical reasons; and no one ever changed from a bad speaker to a good one by applying the rules of grammar to what he said."

The teacher, then, should aim in the class-room to give his pupils such training as will tend to form correct habits of expression. He must remember that language is an expression of thought; and, consequently, that correct thinking should precede expression. The thought of the pupil being clear, the teacher should give frequent opportunities for its expression.

PREFACE.

It is the aim of this book to furnish pupils with such exercises as will give them the necessary practice in expression. For this purpose the daily school work is drawn upon to furnish material for language-lessons. Geography and History, as well as the ordinary reading-lessons and Natural History studies, supply an abundance of such material, and it is hoped that these exercises will prove helpful and suggestive to teachers.

Numerous exercises will be found, in which pupils are led to study *words*, with the expectation that such study will add interest as well as value to the language-work. A study of many of the best poems of American writers is also given, with the hope that, even in the early years of school life, children may learn to love what is purest and best in our own literature.

The selections from Holmes, Longfellow, Lowell, Whittier, and the Cary Sisters, which appear in this book, and the portraits at the head of the chapters in Part III., are used by permission of Messrs. Houghton, Mifflin & Company. We are under a similar obligation to Messrs. D. Appleton & Company, for kindly permitting us to use several selections from the copyright works of William Cullen Bryant. The attention of teachers and pupils is also called to many other poems, which it is hoped they will find time to read. For convenience of reference, a full list of the publications containing the works of the same authors may be found on page 223.

This little book is sent out with a confidence born of many years of experience in the class-room. That it may help to further the language-work now so vigorously prosecuted in most of our schools is the sincere wish of

THE AUTHORS.

PART I.

LANGUAGE EXERCISES.

Chapter One.

LESSON I.

Language.

To the Teacher.—The following lesson should be carefully read in class, and every statement should be fully discussed.

We express our thoughts by means of **language**, sometimes by *speaking*, sometimes by *writing* or *printing*, and sometimes by *signs*.

Spoken, or **oral**, language is addressed to the ear. Written or printed language is addressed to the eye.

Language is made up of sentences, and sentences are made up of words. *Oral words* are made up of sounds, and *written words*, of letters which usually represent sounds.

There are about forty sounds in the different words of our language, and only twenty-six letters to represent them. Some letters must, of course, represent more than one sound; thus, the letter a in the word *fate* has one sound, while in the word *fat* it has another sound, and in the word *far* still another.

The words *bird, dog, horse, cow*, all bring to mind ideas of things that we have seen. The words *noise* and *sound* recall ideas of what we have heard; and *cold, hot, rough,* and *smooth* make us think of what we have felt. A word does not give us an idea of something that we know nothing about; it simply recalls to the mind an idea of something that we have known. Hence we say that *words are signs of ideas.*

LESSON II.
Words.

There are three words in the English language that have only one letter each. Will you name them and use them in sentences?

Some words can be pronounced with one impulse of the voice; as, *boat, ship, cat, bird.* Such words have but one *syllable,* and are called **monosyllables** (*one syllable*).

Some words are pronounced with two impulses of the voice; as, *be-lieve, wor-ship, sen-tence.* Such words are **dissyllables** (*two syllables*).

Words having three syllables are **trisyllables** (*three syllables*); as, *syl-la-ble, im-pul-ses.* Words of more than three syllables are **polysyllables** (*many syllables*); as, *mon-o-syl-la-ble, pol-y-syl-la-ble.*

1. What are monosyllables? Select the monosyllables in the first sentence of this lesson.
2. What are dissyllables? Select the dissyllables in the first sentence of Lesson I.
3. What are trisyllables? Select five trisyllables from Lesson I.

4. What are polysyllables? Find four polysyllables in this lesson.
5. What does the word *teacher* bring to your mind? the word *school? blue? jump?*
6. What is meant by *Words are signs of ideas?*

LESSON III.

Letters.

Letters are divided into *vowels* and *consonants*. A vowel is a letter that represents what is called a pure tone; that is, a tone made by letting the voice flow freely through the organs of speech.

The letters **a, e, i, o, u** are vowels; **y** also is a vowel when it has any one of the sounds of the vowel **i**. No word nor even a syllable of a word can be written without using one of these six letters.

In the word *high*, only the first two letters are sounded. The last two are *silent letters*. In the word *groan, a* is silent. In *are, e* is silent.

NOTE.— W, when heard as in *few* and *cow*, has the sound of $\overline{oo}$, and is a vowel.

1. In the following words, sound each letter and tell whether it is a vowel or a consonant: *crab, from, stem, jump, mind, skip, fond.*
2. Which are the silent letters in *steam, same, walk, sigh, laid, half, calm.*
3. Tell whether *y* is a vowel or a consonant in the following words: *my, yes, fly, yonder, dry.*
4. What five letters are vowels?

LESSON IV.

Vowel Exercises.

1. From the following list, select the words having the same sound of a:

cap, cape, lane, male, fat, man, grate, take, at, have.

How many different sounds has *a* in the ten words?

2. Select the words having the same sound of e:

red, pet, feet, tree, mean, stem, head, steam, see, set.

How many different sounds of *e* in the words?

3. Select the words having the same sound of i:

fine, thine, limb, climb, pine, mine, rip, ripe, win, wine.

How many different sounds of *i* do you find?

4. Select the words having the same sound of o:

note, not, lot, coat, comb, stop, throw, go, got, drove.

How many different sounds of *o* do you find?

5. Select words having the same sound of u:

tune, flute, tub, cut, tube, cube, blunt, hum, thumb, June.

How many different sounds of *u* in these words?

LESSON V.

Vowel Exercises (*Continued*).

In the dictionary, a mark placed above or below a vowel shows what sound should be given to it. This aids us in pronouncing the word correctly.

The two most common marks are the *macron* (-) to show the long sound, and the *breve* (˘) to show the short sound.

The vowels in the following words are correctly marked:

āte, ăt, stēam, stĕm; hīde, hĭd; hōle, hŏt; tūne, tŭb.

Give the long and the short sound of each vowel by itself.

Now write the words in the five lists in Lesson IV., and place a *macron* or a *breve* over the proper letter in each.

To the Teacher. — Pupils should be taught to use a dictionary as soon as possible after entering upon the fourth year of school. The object of such exercises as the foregoing, is to make the pupil familiar with the marks used in the dictionaries to indicate the proper pronunciation of words. When this object is accomplished, further exercises of this kind should be given occasionally for the purpose of review, but should not be allowed to consume time belonging to other work.

NOTE. — In this book the grades are numbered from the lowest (first) grade to the highest.

LESSON VI.

Statements.

To the Teacher. — Ask the pupils to look at their slates and to think about them. Then ask them to tell what they have thought. Select a few of the best expressions, and require the pupils to write them. Something like the following may be the result:

1. My slate was bought more than a month ago.
2. My father bought my slate in Chicago.
3. I dropped my slate upon the floor yesterday.
4. A slate is a very useful article.

To the Teacher. — Exercises like the following should be *oral*, and should lead to familiar conversation with the pupils. After the subject is well understood, pupils may be required to *write* answers to the printed questions.

1. How many thoughts are expressed on your slate?

2. How many groups of words have you used in expressing those thoughts?

3. *A group of words expressing a complete thought* is called a *sentence*. How many *sentences* have you used?

4. *A sentence that states, or tells, something,* is called a *statement.* How many *statements* have you made?

5. With what kind of letter have you begun each sentence?

6. What mark have you placed at the end of each sentence?

LESSON VII.

Questions.

To the Teacher. — Place some object, as, for instance, a *book*, before the class. Ask them to think about it. Let the pupils ask questions about it. Require them to write a few of the most sensible questions. Something like the following may be the result:

1. What is the name of the book?
2. To whom does the book belong?
3. Of what is the book made?
4. How much did the book cost?
5. Where was the book bought?

Answer in oral sentences.

1. Of what were you thinking when you asked the first question? *Ans.* I was thinking of the name of the book.

2. Of what were you thinking when you asked the second question? the third? the fourth? the fifth?

3. What is a *sentence?*

4. Are the five groups of words which you have written sentences? Why?

5. What one name, then, will include both *statements* and *questions?*

6. With what kind of letter does each sentence begin?

7. What mark is placed at the end of each question?

8. Make a rule for the use of capital letters in sentences.

9. Make a rule for the use of the period.

10. Make a rule for the use of the interrogation point.

LESSON VIII.

Study carefully the spelling, capitals, and punctuation in this lesson.

Dictation Exercise.

Deaf and dumb people can neither speak nor hear. They have a sign language. Did you ever see them use this language? Do they talk rapidly with it?
Many deaf mutes have been taught to speak. Then they are no longer mutes.

Answer in complete sentences.

1. Which words in the dictation exercise are dissyllables? Which is a trisyllable? How many monosyllables?

In *rapidly*, why is *y* a vowel? Give a reason for each punctuation mark. Why are the capitals used? What are mutes? What are deaf mutes?

LESSON IX.

Review.

1. Make one *statement* about each of five different things in the room.
2. How many sentences have you used?
3. With what kind of letter does each sentence begin?
4. What mark have you placed after each sentence?
5. Ask five *questions* about the same things.
6. What words in the five questions begin with capital letters, and why?
7. What mark is placed after each question?
8. How many kinds of sentences have you used, and what are their names?

LESSON X.

The Sentence.

Copy the following groups of words, and complete those that are not sentences:

Every thing that breathes is an animal.
An old man in tattered clothing.
When in Boston did you enjoy?
Do little birds have a language?
On Christmas-day should we not remember the poor?
While on my way to school this morning.

1. Tell which of the foregoing groups of words are not sentences, and why they are not.
2. Copy from your reading book five short statements and five questions. Have you copied sentences? How can you tell?
3. Give one rule for the use of capital letters, one for the use of periods, and one for the use of interrogation marks in the sentences which you have copied.

LESSON XI.

Information Exercise.

First, answer each question separately, and then combine each group of answers into one sentence.

1. Give, in one sentence, the names of five animals; of five plants, in another; of five minerals, in another.
2. Do animals grow? move about? breathe? feel? die?
3. Do plants grow? move about? breathe? feel? die?
4. Do minerals grow? move about? breathe? feel? die?

LESSON XII.

Information Exercise.

To the Teacher. — Lessons like this and the preceding are very suggestive, and may require all the time that can be given to language-work for two or three days. Oral exercises should precede written, as pupils should not be required to write what they do not clearly understand.

Refer to Lesson XI. and answer the following questions:

1. How do animals and plants resemble each other?
3. How do animals and plants differ from each other?
2. How do minerals differ from animals?
4. How do minerals differ from plants?
5. How do minerals resemble plants?

A whale, a fly, an elephant, a sparrow, a tiger, a snail, a beetle, a spider, a snake, and a worm are animals that differ widely from one another. Make two statements about each one.

LESSON XIII.

A Story. (*Original.*)

Write a true story about some animal that you have known. Please to note carefully the following suggestions:

a. Be sure that each thought is complete before writing it in a sentence.
b. Be sure to begin each sentence with a capital.
c. Be sure to punctuate every sentence.
d. Write as well as you can.
e. If you have any doubt whatever about the spelling of a word, find it in the dictionary, or ask to have it written on the blackboard.
f. Do not try to write too much.

LESSON XIV.

Information Exercise.

First *oral* and then *written.*

1. Are birds, fishes, and insects animals?
2. Which do you think are the five most useful animals?
3. Tell why each is useful?
4. What is the largest animal that you have seen?
5. Of what use, if any, is he to man?
6. Tell a story that you have heard or read about this animal.

To the Teacher. — It is expected that very many questions will be asked and answered during the discussion of such lessons as the foregoing. *Demand complete statements for all answers.* New or difficult words should be written upon the blackboard. Such lessons should stimulate children to find out things for themselves. Hence, close the lesson with questions to be answered next day.

LESSON XV.

Information Exercise.

1. Name five important food plants.
2. Which plant do you think feeds the most people?
3. Name three plants that are useful for clothing.
4. What is the largest plant that you have seen?
5. Give some of its uses.
6. Name some plants that are cultivated only because they are beautiful.
7. Do you think such plants are useful?

LESSON XVI.

Information Exercise.

Some minerals are called metals. Gold, silver, copper, mercury, lead, tin, etc. are metals.

1. Name six useful metals.
2. Which do you think most useful? Give reasons.
3. How are minerals usually obtained?
4. Brass is made from two other metals. What are they?
5. From what is steel made?
6. From what mineral is window glass made?

LESSON XVII.

Dictation and Classification.

Study spelling, capitals, and punctuation.

Dictation Exercise.

Every thing in the world is either *animal, vegetable,* or *mineral.* Things that we get from animals are called animal productions. Things that we get from plants are called vegetable productions. Every thing else is mineral. So there are only three classes of objects. When we say a thing is animal, vegetable, or mineral, we *classify* it.

Classification Exercise.

Classify the objects named below, thus: Corn is a vegetable production.

salt	cotton	leather	hair
pepper	stone	bread	milk
eggs	coffee	ivory	water
ribbon	butter	candy	paper

LANGUAGE EXERCISES.

LESSON XVIII.
Story from a Picture.

Write a story from the picture above, using the following hints:

The little boy and girl that you see in the picture are brother and sister. Where do they live? Do you think they are playing truant, or is it a holiday? Which is older, the boy or the girl, and what are their names?

They have been out playing and have found a strange dog. I wonder what has happened to him! They found him lying by the side of the road and crying piteously. He looked up at them as though he would like to tell them what had happened. The children could hear the noise of a carriage that had just been driven by. Has he been run over, or has he been bitten by another dog? What are the children trying to do? Why do they pity the poor dog?

When they have bound up the poor dog's foot, do you suppose they will take him to their own home? What a nice playfellow he will make if he gets well!

LESSON XIX.
Pronunciation and Classification.

Pronounce very distinctly the following words according to the marking:

whōle	slēēk	ĕlm	wĭdōw
nōbŏdў	băde	pĕtal	hŏrrĭd
drāin	pātrĭŏt	fōrge	sĭttĭng
mĭnnōws	vĭctōrў	does (oe=ŭ)	hăppĭnĕss

Write in separate columns the monosyllables, the dissyllables, and the trisyllables, arranging the words in each column alphabetically.

Use each word in an oral sentence, speaking very distinctly.

LESSON XX.

Commit the following selection to memory, studying the meaning of each sentence:

A WORD TO BOYS.

You are made to be kind, boys, — generous, magnanimous. If there is a boy in school who has a club-foot, don't let him know you ever saw it. If there is a poor boy with ragged clothes, don't talk about rags in his hearing. If there is a lame boy, assign him some part in the game that doesn't require running. If there is a hungry one, give him part of your dinner. If there is a dull one, help him get his lesson. If there is a bright one, be not envious of him; for if one boy is proud of his talents, and another is envious of them, there are two great wrongs, and no more talent than before. If a boy has injured you, and is sorry for it, forgive him. All the school will show by their countenances how much better it is than to have a great fuss. — HORACE MANN.

To the Teacher. — One or two conversation lessons may well be had upon the foregoing extract. Be sure that each sentence has suggested its appropriate thought.

CHAPTER TWO.

LESSON I.

Proper Names.

THE name of a particular person, place or thing is called a *proper name*, or *proper noun;* as, John, Chicago, England.

Dictation Exercise.

Write the following sentences, and then select the proper nouns. Notice carefully the spelling and capital letters.

1. Sleepy Hollow is near the Hudson River.
2. Is not Bunker Hill in Boston?
3. The home of George Washington was in Virginia.
4. In what State is the city of New York?
5. The capital of the United States is on the Potomac.
6. Benjamin Franklin lived in Philadelphia.
7. George Washington was inaugurated President of the United States on April 30, 1789, at New York.

Oral Exercise on the foregoing sentences.

1. Give reasons for the punctuation.
2. Which proper nouns contain more than one word?
3. Make a rule for writing each word in the proper names.
4. Classify the words in the proper names according to the number of syllables.
5. Select the *statements* in the dictation exercise.
6. Select the *questions*.
7. Change the first statement into a question.
8. Change the first question into a statement.
9. Tell some story about George Washington.
10. State two or more facts about Benjamin Franklin.

LESSON II.

Proper Names (*Continued*).

1. Write five sentences, each containing the name of a boy and the name of the place where he lives.
2. Write the same of five girls whom you know.
3. Write a short account of a visit to one of these boys or girls.

NOTE. — Read the suggestions in Lesson XIII., Chapter One, before writing.

LESSON III.

Names and Dates.

Oral and then *written.*

Be sure of the capitals and of the spelling of the words that you will use in writing the answers to the following questions:

Answer in complete sentences and use no abbreviations.

1. When is your birthday?
2. On what date is Christmas?
3. Which is the shortest month?
4. Which months have thirty-one days?
5. Which months have thirty days?
6. Which is the middle day of the week?
7. On which days is there no school?
8. On which day of the week are your lessons poorest?
9. When is Washington's birthday?
10. On what date are you answering this question?

Make a new rule for the use of capitals.

LESSON IV.

Story from a Picture.

Write a story from this picture. The girl, the boy, and the dog are the same that you saw on page 12.

Suggestions.

What have the children been doing? Was it good fun? Did the sticks float down the stream? What did Carlo do? How long had they been playing?

What was the little girl trying to do when she fell off the bridge? Was the water very deep? Why did Carlo plunge into the water after the little girl? Could the brother help her? Did mamma and papa hear him when he called? What might have happened?

Was the little girl sick for a long time? I wonder whether Carlo used to go into the sick-room to see her? Was she glad that they had so good a dog? Do you suppose that papa and mamma were sorry that the children had taken pity on the poor, lame dog?

LESSON V.

Vowel Sounds.

Some of the vowels have other sounds besides the long and the short sounds.

The letter *a* has a different sound in each of these words: cāne, căn, tạll, fär, ȧsk.

You know the names of the first two sounds of *a*. The third is called *broad a,* and the fourth *Italian a*. The fifth sound is the hardest of all to learn. It is just midway between *short a* and *Italian a*. It should be heard in such words as ȧsk, grȧss, brȧnch, dȧnce, glȧss, tȧsk.

1. Tell which of the following words have *broad a* and which have *Italian a :* far, fall, are, palm, talk, all, star, squall, mark, hard? Mark the *a* in each word.

2. Write five other words containing broad *a,* and five containing Italian *a*.

LESSON VI.

Vowel Sounds (*Continued*).

The sound of o in mọve, of oo in mōōn, and of u in rụde, are all exactly alike. The sound is called *long oo*, and the vowels are marked as you see them.

The sounds of o in wọlf, oo in fo͝ot, and u in bụll, are all alike. The sound is called *short oo*.

1. Pronounce the following words with the *long oo* sound, and tell how the vowels should be marked: whose, soon, true, prove, do, room, fruit, canoe, rule, brute.

2. Pronounce the following words with the *short oo* sound, and tell how the vowels should be marked: push, good, foot, pull, woman.

3. Review Lesson V.

LESSON VII.

Information Exercise.

Study the following description of the fly until you can write it correctly from dictation:

THE FLY.

The fly is an insect, and so it has six legs and its body seems to be almost cut into three parts. On its head it has two large eyes; and if you could look at it through a strong glass, you would see that each eye is made up of a great many small eyes.

It has two wings, with which it can fly; and the wings move so fast that they hum when the fly darts through the air.

It has three pair of legs, and with them it can walk or run; but it does not jump.

Its feet are so made that it can walk up a wall or a pane of glass, or even crawl on the flat ceiling of a room.

Wood's "Natural History Reader."

NOTE. — The teacher may find it convenient to divide the dictation exercise above into two short ones. Similar extracts, containing valuable information, may be selected and dictated to the class.

A few judicious conversation and observation lessons on the "Fly" will prepare the pupils for the language lessons which follow.

Consult elementary works on Natural History, and, if possible, lead the children to examine specimens with the aid of magnifying glasses.

Conversation Exercise.

Suggestions.

Tell what you know about each topic below. Be sure that your thoughts are properly expressed in sentences.

1. The fly, an insect. Why? Its eyes, legs, feet, trunk.
2. The egg — the grub — the hard shell.
3. When the fly stops growing.
4. How the fly eats.
5. How it keeps itself clean.

LESSON VIII.

Composition.

Write a description of a fly, following the order of the "Suggestions" in Lesson VII. Add anything of interest that you have learned.

LESSON IX.

Words and their *Opposites*.

1. What are the opposites of *rough, sweet, brittle, long, up, right, east, north, swift, best?*

2. Write sentences each of which shall contain one of the foregoing words and its opposite.

Accented Syllables.

Words of more than one syllable have what is called an accented syllable; that is, a syllable which is pronounced with a stronger impulse of the voice than the others in the same word. Thus, in the words *yesterday, playing,* and *garden,* the first syllables are accented. In the dictionaries such syllables are marked as follows:

yes'ter day   play'ing   gar'den

3. Separate the following words into syllables, and mark the accented syllable in each :—*delay, honest, becoming, syllable, others, belong, incomplete, believe, follow.*

Review.

1. Arrange the words, in the list above, alphabetically.
2. Classify them as to syllables.
3. Mark the accented vowel in each word to indicate its sound.
4. Is *y* a vowel or a consonant in the word *syllable?* Why?

LESSON X.

Dictation Exercise.

Study carefully the spelling, capitals, and punctuation of the following exercise:

To the Teacher. — Dictate each sentence distinctly and but once.

Bunker Hill is in Boston, the capital of Massachusetts. The battle of Bunker Hill was fought in June, 1775. The Americans fought on one side, and the British on the other. The British troops were assisted by the ships in the Charles River. Were the British or the Americans, victorious? Where is Bunker Hill Monument?

1. Arrange in a column and separate into syllables all the dissyllables, marking the accented syllable of each word.

2. Arrange and mark in the same way the trisyllables; the polysyllables.

3. Give reasons for the use of periods and question marks in the dictation exercise above.

LESSON XI.

Pronunciation.

Pronounce distinctly the following words as they are marked:

clȧss	brŏn chī′ tĭs	re cĕss′
heärth	kĕt′tle	chĭl′dren
rōōt	stămp′ing	chȧnce
sau̩′cy	rōōf′less	ba nä′na

1. Use each word in an oral sentence.

2. Arrange all the words alphabetically, and mark, from memory, the accented vowels as in the dictionary.

LANGUAGE EXERCISES. 21

LESSON XII.

Dictation Exercise.

Study carefully the following sentences, and find out the answers to the questions:

To the Teacher.—Require each question to be written after one reading, and then have the answer written in a complete sentence.

1. On what date is (or was) Easter Sunday this year?
2. What occurs the first Monday of every December?
3. What takes place, every fourth year, on the first Tuesday after the first Monday in November?
4. How many days between Ash-Wednesday and Easter Sunday?
5. What usually comes the last Thursday of November?
6. What is the Friday before Easter called?
7. Can there ever be five Saturdays in February? Explain.

LESSON XIII.

Oral and then *written.*

Fill each of the following blanks with *is* or *are:*

1. Every one of the horses .... lame.
2. John and Mary .... going with me.
3. John or Mary .... going with me.
4. Each of the children .... to receive a book.
5. One of those books .... mine.

Use *was* or *were* in each of the foregoing sentences.
Complete the following sentences with *I, me, he,* or *him:*

1. Between you and .... it is not fair for him to say so.
2. He can read better than .... but I can write better than .....
3. I did not know that it was .... who broke the window.
4. Mother gave the candy to .... and .....

LESSON XIV.

Seeds and Plants.

Oral and then *written.*

1. In what season of the year does the farmer plant seed?
2. Mention a few of the kinds of seed that he plants.
3. How must the ground be prepared before planting?
4. Of what use is the root of the plant?
5. Why does a very large tree have very large roots?
6. Mention a small plant that has a large root.
7. Name some roots that are good to eat.
8. Of what use are the leaves of a plant?
9. Are the leaves ever used for food?

Composition.

Write all that the foregoing questions suggest to you about *seeds* and *plants.*

LESSON XV.

1. Pronounce the following words as they are marked:

rule	vī'o let	cătch
sĭn'gu lar	hŭn' drĕd	ŏff
be cause'	glánce	pa pä'
bŏn'net	nō'bod y	mam mä'

2. Use each word in a complete oral sentence which shall show that you know its meaning.
3. Classify the words according to the number of syllables.

Written.

1. Use each word in a sentence.
2. Which words are accented on the first syllable?
3. Which words have no accent? Why?
4. Which words are accented on the last syllable?

LESSON XVI.

Stanzas, Verses, and Rhymes.

To the Teacher.—Select a poem from the class Reader. Require the pupils to study it carefully, and then to answer the following questions:

Answers in oral sentences.

1. How many *stanzas* in the poem?
2. How many lines in each stanza?
3. Each line begins with what kind of letter?
4. Each line of poetry is one *verse*. How many verses in each stanza?
5. How many verses in the poem?
6. In the first stanza select two verses that *rhyme*.
7. How can you tell whether verses rhyme or not?
8. Please turn to a lesson in *prose*. How does it differ in appearance from the poetry?
9. Make a special rule for capitals in poetry.

LESSON XVII.

Stanzas, Verses, and Rhymes (*Continued*).

Study carefully the following stanzas, as to verses, capitals, punctuation, and spelling. Study also what the authors wish to suggest to us.

Dictation Exercise.

"Great God, my Father and my Friend,
 On whom I cast my constant care,
On whom for all things I depend,
 To thee I raise my humble prayer."

"The unwearied sun, from day to day,
 Does his Creator's power display,
And publishes to every land
 The work of an Almighty hand."

Oral Exercise.

1. How many verses have you written?
2. Select the verses that rhyme.
3. What names in the stanzas begin with capitals?
4. Why should those words begin with capitals?
5. Make a rule for writing such words.
6. What other capitals have you used, and why?
7. What is meant by "the *unwearied* sun" and "from day to day?"
8. What does the sun display? How?
9. What does the third verse of the second stanza mean?
10. Does the sun shine upon every land every day?

LESSON XVIII.

Commit to memory the following poem, studying at the same time to get the best thought out of it:

THE WIND AND THE LEAVES.

1. "Come little leaves," said the wind one day,
 "Come o'er the meadows with me, and play.
 Put on your dresses of red and gold; —
 Summer is gone, and the days grow cold."

2. Soon as the leaves heard the wind's low call,
 Down they came fluttering, one and all;
 Over the brown fields they danced and flew,
 Singing the soft little songs they knew.

3. "Cricket, good-by, we've been friends so long!
 Pretty brook, sing us your farewell song; —
 Say you are sorry to see us go.
 Oh! you will miss us, right well we know.

4. "Dear little lambs, in your fleecy fold,
Mother will keep you from harm and cold;
Fondly we've watched you in vale and glade:
Say, will you dream of our loving shade?"

5. Dancing and whirling, the little leaves went:
Winter had called them, and they were content.
Soon fast asleep in their earthly beds,
The snow laid a coverlet over their heads.

LESSON XIX.

Study of Poem.

Answers to be oral sentences.

1. In the first stanza of "The Wind and the Leaves," who is speaking?
2. What was the time of year? How do you know?
3. About how old were the leaves?
4. What were the "dresses of red and gold"? At whose bidding did they put them on? What dresses did they lay off?
5. How did the leaves "sing little songs"?
6. In the third stanza, who is speaking?
7. Why should the cricket and the leaves have been friends? the leaves and the brook? the leaves and the lambs?
8. How does a brook sing? Did you ever hear one? Where?
9. What is a "fleecy fold"? Do lambs dream?
10. What is meant by "vale and glade"?
11. How had winter called the leaves? In what sort of bed did they sleep? Did they ever wake up?
12. What becomes of all the leaves year after year?

LESSON XX.

Composition on Leaves.

Oral one day and *written* the next.

Divide your composition into two parts, — leaves in spring and summer, and leaves in autumn and winter. Follow the order of the questions below.

When do the leaves come out? What is their color then? How does it change as summer comes on? Of what use are the leaves to the tree? Of what other uses are they?

When do the leaves put on bright colors? What causes them to do so? How long do their dresses of red and gold last? What happens then? Are the leaves of any further use?

Rules convenient for reference.

Rule 1. — The first word of every sentence should begin with a capital letter.

Rule 2. — A period should be placed at the end of a complete statement; as, *This book is mine.*

Rule 3. — An interrogation-point should be placed at the end of a sentence which asks a question; as, *Are you going to the lecture this evening?*

Rule 4. — Every word in proper names should begin with a capital; as, *George Washington, Mary Stuart, Boston, Chicago.*

Rule 5. — The names of the days of the week and of the months of the year should begin with capitals.

Rule 6. — The first word in every line of poetry should begin with a capital.

Rule 7. — All names applied to God should begin with capitals.

Chapter Three.

LESSON I.

Paragraphs.

For convenience, books are divided into chapters, and chapters are divided into paragraphs.

A paragraph is a division of a chapter which relates to some particular part of the subject upon which the author is writing. Thus, the first two lines of this chapter form a paragraph.

The first word of a paragraph is usually set in, or *indented*, to the right of the first words in the lines above and below it.

It would be much more difficult to read books if they were not divided into chapters and paragraphs. This you will easily understand if you will try to read some one's composition that has not been divided into paragraphs.

A *paragraph* should contain all that relates to some particular part of a topic. If you will examine the paragraphs in any carefully written book, you can tell what the author is writing about in each one.

There are usually two or more sentences in a paragraph, but it may contain only one. It must be remembered that all the sentences in a paragraph should express thoughts which are closely related to each other.

LANGUAGE EXERCISES.

Answer in oral sentences.

1. How many paragraphs are there on the preceding page?
2. How many lines are indented? What do you understand by *indented?*
3. What is the first paragraph about? the second? the third? the fourth? the fifth?
4. Why should letters and other kinds of composition be divided into paragraphs?
5. How can you tell when to begin a new paragraph?

LESSON II.

Dictation Exercise.

Children are fond of strolling along the shore of any large body of water. They like to gather shells from the sand and to wade in the water.

The shells which they find are of various sizes, colors, and shapes. The insides of the shells are always smooth, and sometimes they are very beautiful. Perhaps you can tell something about those which you have gathered. It will be better still, to bring them to school and examine them together.

Did you ever think, children, that every shell has been the home of a living creature?

Answer in complete sentences.

1. How many paragraphs in the dictation exercise?
2. Why should there be just that number of paragraphs?
3. What is the first paragraph about? the second? the third?
4. Give a reason for the use of each period and of each question mark.
5. Answer the question in the last paragraph.

LANGUAGE EXERCISES. 29

LESSON III.

Pronounce the following words according to the marking:

ac cĕnt'ed   băl lōōn'   băl' us ter
a gainst'(g̃ĕnst) bọu quet' (kā)   băl'us trāde
ạl'wāyṣ   çĕl' lar   eū' po là
ā' prĭ cŏt   eŏr' al   grĭ māce'

1. Arrange the words alphabetically.
2. Classify them as to their syllables.
3. Use each word in a sentence which shall clearly show that you know its correct meaning.

Most people mispronounce some of the words in the columns above, and very few can use them *all* correctly. Please study this lesson carefully.

To the Teacher. — Accept nothing but thoughtful sentences. Those that are suggested by the children's experiences or reading are the best.

LESSON IV.
Oral Exercise.

To the Teacher. — The following questions are intended to be only suggestive. All *oral* exercises should be conversation exercises.

BRICKS.

1. Have you ever seen a brick-yard?
2. Of what are bricks made?
3. What is a brick-kiln?
4. Why are not bricks that are baked in the sun as good as those baked in a kiln?
5. What are some of the uses of bricks?
6. What is the man called who builds houses of bricks?
7. What is the shape of a brick, and how large are they usually made?
8. Which do you think are better for the building of houses, bricks or stones? Why?

LESSON V.

Composition on Bricks.

Write what you have learned about *bricks*, making use of the questions in Lesson IV. as hints.

Add one paragraph which shall contain all that you have learned from the Bible about brick-making in the olden time.

Read Lesson I. before writing, and be careful in deciding how many paragraphs you will have.

LESSON VI.

Incomplete Sentences.

First *oral* and then *written*.

Fill each blank in the following sentences with one of these words: *this, these, them, that, those.*

1. What is .... in your hand?
2. .... is a knife.
3. Are .... pencils that I see on your desk?
4. Yes, I am sharpening ....
5. Do you think .... knife is better than .... one?
6. Certainly, and .... pencils are better than .... on your desk.
7. Why are .... better than .... on my desk?
8. .... on your desk are not sharpened at all, while .... are all ready for use.
9. .... will be sharpened as well as ..... I shall sharpen .... with .... knife.
10. .... knife and .... pencils will keep you busy for some time.

Write ten sentences, using each of the words in the list above twice.

LESSON VII.

Reproduction.

Read the following story carefully once or twice. Do not try to remember the sentences, but try to understand them. Then close your book and think how you could tell the story in your own words without using the word *I*. Add one paragraph of your own, telling what you think of the bird's act.

TRUE STORY OF A FISH-HAWK.

When I was a little girl I lived in Virginia, near the Potomac River. One sunny May morning my father said, "Come, Elinor, I want you to go with me." In a few minutes I was on my pony's back. We took the road by the river. The birds were singing merrily, and delicate wild-flowers timidly looked out into this great world. As we came near the woods, the air was filled with smoke, and we could see the flames creeping among the dead leaves on the ground.

We stopped our horses. What strange cry was that we heard? It came from a bird above us, flying slowly round and round. What is the trouble? Ah! We can see a tall tree-trunk by the roadside. In the topmost branches is a nest, and around it the bird is flying. Her little brood are there. The flames are even now running up a dead vine that clings to the trunk. Some of the twigs of the nest are on fire. The bird stops her cries, flies swiftly to the nest, and pulls out the burning twigs with her beak. But she cannot pull them out fast enough. The little birds must burn. What will the mother-bird do? She quietly folds her wings over her little ones, and dies with them.

To the Teacher. — The oral exercise should prove that the children have a clear conception of the story and of the sentences which they will use in telling it. They should be able to make a vivid word-picture of the scene, telling just how everything looked.

LESSON VIII.

Abbreviations and Initials.

Some words are shortened in writing, — two or three letters only representing the whole word; as, Col. for Colonel; Esq. for Esquire; Hon. for Honorable, and Rev. for Reverend. Col., Esq., Hon., and Rev. are called *abbreviations*.

The first letter of a word is called the *initial* letter. When we speak of a person's *initials*, we mean the letters beginning the words in his name; thus, J. A. B. are the *initials* of James Addison Barrett. Such initials are abbreviations, and should be treated as such.

Learn the following abbreviations and use them in sentences of your own.

@, *at.*
A. M. (*Ante Meridiem*) *Before noon.*
Av., *Avenue.*
Capt., *Captain.*
Col., *Colonel.*
cts., *cents.*
doz., *dozen.*
Esq., *Esquire.*
etc. (*Et cætera*), *and so forth.*

Gen., *General.*
M. (Meridian), *Noon.*
Mrs., *Mistress.*
P. M. (*Post Meridiem*) *Afternoon.*
P. M., *Postmaster.*
P. O., *Post-Office.*
P. S., *Postscript.*
Rev., *Reverend.*
St., *Street.*

To the Teacher. — After an oral recitation, pronounce the words as in a spelling-lesson, and require the proper abbreviations to be written by the pupils.

LESSON IX.

Study carefully the abbreviations, spelling, capitals, and punctuation of the following exercise. As a preparation, copy the abbreviations in Lesson VIII., and then write from memory the words for which they stand.

LANGUAGE EXERCISES.

Dictation Exercise.

1. Gen. U. S. Grant died July 23, 1885.
2. The morning session of school begins at 9 o'clock A. M. and closes at 12 M.
3. Col. James A. Dean was seen on Lincoln Av., at 2 o'clock P. M.
4. Capt. and Mrs. Barry are living at 312 Arlington St.
5. Rev. H. W. Beecher died March 8, 1887.
6. Samuel Weller added a P. S. to his letter, and then took it to the P. O.
7. 6 doz. eggs @ 12 cts. a doz. will cost 72 cts.
8. A *company* of soldiers is commanded by a captain, a *regiment* by a colonel, and an *army* by a general.
9. Benjamin Disraeli was created a peer for eminent services, with the title of Earl Beaconsfield.

Oral Exercise.

1. What titles are used in the dictation exercise in connection with the names of persons?
2. What titles are not so used?
3. What titles are abbreviated in the sentences which you have written?
4. What titles are not abbreviated?
5. What titles begin with capital letters?
6. What titles do not begin with capital letters?
7. Make a rule for the use of capitals in titles.
8. What initials are used as abbreviations? Should such initials be capitals?
9. What mark should be placed after every abbreviation?
10. What is a postscript? What is the abbreviation for "*and so forth.*"
11. What was the highest office held by Gen. U. S. Grant?

NOTE. — The sign @ is usually written without the period.

LESSON X.
Sounds of Consonants.

The consonants b, d, f, h, j, k, l, m, p, q, r, t, v, w, y, z, are never marked in the dictionary, because they always stand for the same or (in the case of d as in chafed) for nearly the same sounds.

In *cent* the sound of c is soft, or like the sound of s. In *can* the sound of c is hard, or like the sound of k. The letter is marked thus: çent, ean.

In *gentle* the sound of g is soft like the sound of j. In *get* the sound of g is hard. The letter is marked thus: ġentle, ġet.

In *sun*, the sound of s is sharp. When s stands for this sound it is not marked in the dictionary.

In *rising*, s has the sound of z, and is said to be *vocal*, because the voice is heard in the sound. When it stands for this sound the s is marked thus: riṣing.

Oral Exercise.

1. Give the sounds of the consonants that are never marked.
2. In the following words is the sound of c hard or soft? — *cellar, caller, cinder, curve, ceiling, circle, cut, curl.*
3. How would you mark c in each word?
4. In the following words is the sound of g hard or soft? — *go, gave, general, genius, gander, German, great.*
5. How would you mark g in each word?
6. In the following words, is the sound of s sharp or vocal? — *this, his, sons, say, miss, sees, seem, miser, hers, sinners.*
7. In which words would you mark the s? Which words have both the sharp and the vocal sound of s?
8. How would you mark the c, g, and s in the following words? — *grass, gems, circle, crags, sense, singe, cries, nice.*

LESSON XI.

Story from a Picture.

Oral one day and *written* the next.

Connect a story with the picture below, and arrange your composition in four paragraphs:

Suggestions.

Robins — season of year — where they have been all winter — they are glad to get back — where is the tree?

Building the nest — lining it — eggs — number and color.

The baby birds — how they look — how long they live in the nest — how they are fed — how they are taught to fly.

Why we should be kind to the birds — the pleasure they give — their happy and useful lives.

To the Teacher. — One or two oral lessons, skillfully conducted, will prepare the pupils for the written composition.

LESSON XII.

Common Nouns. Singular and Plural.

In Chapter Two, Lesson I., we spoke of proper names, or proper nouns. There is another kind of name. The word *dog* may be applied to any dog in the world; therefore we say it is a common name, or common noun. For the same reason such words as *book* and *slate* are common nouns.

1. Select the common nouns from the following list, and tell why they are *common:* door, window, Mary, pencil, Ralph, stove, apple, Columbus, Webster, orange.

Names that mean but *one* are said to be *singular*. Names that mean *more than one* are said to be *plural*. *Door, window,* and *pencil* are singular; but *doors, windows,* and *pencils* are plural.

2. Tell whether the following common nouns are singular or plural, and why: *man, horses, child, doors, robins, children, boys, kite, knives, apple, girl, woman, foxes, oxen.*

3. Use the foregoing nouns in sentences.

To the Teacher. — Select a lesson from the Reader, and require the pupils to tell whether the nouns are common or proper, singular or plural.

LESSON XIII.

Learn to spell the following plural nouns:

chimneys	pianos	babies	journeys
knives	potatoes	wives	candies
ponies	valleys	scissors	ladies
children	oxen	women	glasses

1. Try to use the singular of each noun in a sentence.
2. Rewrite your sentences, using the plural noun

instead of the singular, and making such other changes as are necessary.

3. Is *scissors* ever used in the singular? Name another noun used only in the plural.

LESSON XIV.

Write the following story as though there were two squirrels instead of one, and use *we* instead of *I:*

THE SQUIRREL.

A little red squirrel lives in a tree near our home and we are getting to be quite good friends. When I first saw him, he was on a limb of the tree just over my head, and what a noise he did make! I think he was trying to tell me to go away.

I put two or three nuts on the ground near the tree, and he soon came and picked them up. You ought to have seen how funny he looked with two large nuts in his mouth.

The next day I went and left some more nuts in the same place, and he came and picked them up while I was standing near by. In a few days he would come and take the nuts from my hand, jump upon my shoulder, and then leap into the tree.

Now when I go near his tree, I find him watching for me. He will run to meet me, jump into my arms, and look into all my pockets for something to eat.

LESSON XV.

Oral and then written.

1. Make a statement beginning with *There is.* One beginning with *There are.*

2. Make the same statement without using the word *there.*

3. Ask a question beginning with *Are you.* One beginning with *Were you.*
4. Make a statement beginning with *There was.* One beginning with *There were.*
5. Make the same statement without using *there.*
6. Ask a question beginning with *Is there.* One beginning with *Are there.*
7. Make a statement beginning with *You are.* One beginning with *You were.*
8. Ask a question beginning with *Was there.* One beginning with *Were there.*

Note.—Teachers will find it necessary to review frequently such lessons as the one above.

LESSON XVI.

Information Exercise.

Study the following description of a spider until you can write it in your own words, without help from the book:

THE SPIDER.

Spiders are not insects. Most people think that a spider is an insect, but they are quite wrong.

An insect looks as if its body were almost cut into three parts; and it always has six legs. Now the body of the spider is made up of two pieces joined together, and it has eight legs.

Insects always go through a number of changes after they are hatched; but the spiders have no such change. A young spider is of the same shape as an old one.

All spiders spin webs, while no insect can spin a web of any kind. Wood's "Natural History Reader."

These are some of the reasons why we say that spiders are not insects. Can you find out other reasons?

LESSON XVII.

Conversation Exercise.

To the Teacher. — Talk with the pupils about the Spider. Encourage them to examine it themselves, and to gather such information as they can by their own efforts. The following suggestions may be of assistance. They will furnish material for several lessons, if wisely used.

Suggestions.

Not a true insect. Why? Body divided into two parts. Number of legs. How it breathes. Insects go through what changes? Webs, — how made. Different kinds of spiders, — wolf spiders, — hunting spiders, — mason spiders, — field spiders, — water spiders. How water spiders build their nests. How garden spiders spin their webs. How they catch their prey.

Written Exercise.

1. Name an insect. Into how many parts is its body divided? How many legs has it? How does it breathe? What changes does it go through during its life?

2. Into how many parts is the body of a spider divided? How many legs has it? How does a spider breathe? Does it spin a web?

3. Then why is not the spider an insect?

4. What kinds of spiders have you studied? What is the most interesting spider that you have studied? State some facts about this spider.

LESSON XVIII.

Composition.

Write a composition on the "Spider," following the order of the "Suggestions" in Lesson XVII., and dividing your composition into three paragraphs.

LESSON XIX.

Study and commit to memory the following poem:

BOYS WANTED.

1. Boys of spirit, boys of will,
   Boys of muscle, brain, and power,
   Fit to cope with anything,—
   These are wanted every hour.

2. Not the weak and whining drones
   Who all troubles magnify,—
   Not the watchword of "I•can't,"
   But the nobler one, "I'll try."

3. Do whate'er you have to do,
   With a true and earnest zeal;
   Bend your sinews to the task,—
   "Put your shoulder to the wheel."

4. Though your duty may be hard,
   Look not on it as an ill;
   If it be an honest task,
   Do it with an honest will.

5. In the workshop, on the farm,
   Or wherever you may be,
   From your future efforts, boys,
   Comes a nation's destiny.

LESSON XX.

Oral Exercise on "Boys Wanted."

1. Give a description of the boys, and tell what is meant.
2. What does the third verse in the first stanza mean?

3. " These are wanted every hour " where and by whom?
4. What is meant by " whining drones "?
5. What is it to magnify troubles? What is the opposite?
6. What is a watchword?
7. May there be a difference between *earnest* zeal and *true* zeal?
8. What are " your sinews "?
9. " Put your shoulder " to what wheel? Why your *shoulder?*
10. Give your thought of the fourth stanza.
11. Is the boy in the workshop as good as any other?
12. Which would you prefer, to have nothing to do, or to earn your own bread?
13. What do the last two lines mean? Do you believe what they say?
14. What *nation* is meant?
15. Do the boys spoken of in the poem mean the boys in this very school?
16. Do you love your country? What is a patriot?
17. Do you love to read about patriots?
18. How can every boy make his country better and stronger?
19. Can you name one boy who will try to do it?

Chapter Four.

LESSON I.

The Apostrophe.

We have already learned that words used as names are called *nouns*, and that nouns are sometimes singular and sometimes plural.

A noun can be written so as to denote ownership; as, *Mary's sponge cost ten cents. James's pony is at his uncle's farm.* Here Mary owns the sponge, and James owns the pony.

If the noun is *singular*, we add the apostrophe and the letter *s* as in the sentences above.

If the noun is *plural* and does not end in *s*, it is made to denote ownership in the same way; as, *The children's vacation will begin next Saturday. The men's clothing was ruined by the fire.*

If the noun is *plural* and ends in *s*, the apostrophe only is added; as, *The soldiers' uniforms are blue. The boys' hats were on the girls' heads.*

First *oral* and then *written*.

1. In the foregoing sentences, in italics, what nouns are made to express ownership by adding an apostrophe and *s?*

2. What nouns are made to express ownership by adding the apostrophe only?

3. What plural nouns are made to express ownership in the same way as singular nouns?

4. Use each of the following nouns in a sentence so as to denote ownership: *man, men, dogs, horses, woman, women.*

LESSON II.

Dictation Exercise.

WILLIE'S FIRST VISIT TO THE FARM.

One pleasant evening in July, Willie arrived at his uncle's farm. He was tired out by a long day's journey, and soon went to bed. The next morning he fed Aunt Lizzie's hens and chickens. After dinner he drove his uncle's horse to the Post-office. On the way home he called at cousin George's store and bought some tea, coffee, and sugar.

Answer in oral sentences.

1. Select all the nouns in the dictation exercise. Which of them are plural?
2. Which nouns are begun with capitals? Why?
3. Which nouns denote ownership? Why is the apostrophe placed before the *s* in each of these nouns?
4. Select all the words of more than one syllable.
5. What name is given to words of one syllable?
6. What is meant by the word *uncle? aunt? cousin?*

LESSON III.

For Oral Reproduction.

THE GOOSE AND THE GOLDEN EGGS.

A FABLE.

1. Once on a time there was a man who had a goose he thought a great deal of. And well he might do so, for this was the strangest goose that ever lived.
2. Every day she laid an egg. "There is nothing strange

about that," you will say. Ah! but the eggs this goose laid were of solid gold. Think of that!

3. Day after day this strange bird laid a shining golden egg for her master. That was why he liked the goose so much. You may be sure he did not sell these eggs in the market. Not he: he hid them away carefully in a great iron box.

4. Every day he found a bright new golden egg in the goose's nest, and added it to the pile. He was so glad to get it that he could hardly wait for the night to pass and the morning to come. Each day seemed as long as a week to him.

5. When he saw the pile growing higher and higher in the iron box, he rubbed his hands with glee. "Ah!" said he to himself, "if it were only full, I should be the richest man in the world."

6. He could think of nothing but his golden pile. At last he grew so greedy that he wanted all his gold at once. He thought he would find plenty of eggs in the goose's body, and not have to wait and wait and wait any longer.

7. So one day he killed the wonderful bird. But when he came to look for more eggs, — why, there were none to be found!

Foolish man! He had killed the goose that laid the golden eggs.

To the Teacher. — The first lesson on this fable should be conversation. The story should be told two or three times by the pupils, many of them taking part. Insist upon clear sentences and distinct utterance. The children should understand what a fable is, and for what purpose it is written. They should, of course, be able to deduce the lesson from it.

LESSON IV.

Composition.

Write, in your own words, the story of "The Goose and the Golden Eggs."

LANGUAGE EXERCISES. 45

LESSON V.

The Apostrophe (*Continued*).

First *oral* and then *written*.

1. Use the following names in sentences: *girl's, girls'; boy's, boys'; church's, churches'; man's men's; mouse's mice's; pony's, ponies'*.

2. Use each of the following names in a sentence in such a way as to require the addition of the apostrophe and the letter *s*; *aunt, uncle, brother, sister, cousin, Bessy, Mr. Davis*.

3. Complete the following sentences with names denoting ownership:

Is that Mr. .... house? No, it is Mrs. .....
This is .... knife but that one is .....
Mr. .... horse, Mr. .... cows, and Mr. .... sheep are in one pasture.

LESSON VI.

Dictation Exercise.

Study the spelling and punctuation of the following sentences:

A teacher once sent four pupils, viz., John, Fred, Mary, and Martha, to examine a large tree standing near the school-house.

When they returned, each reported as follows: John told of the size of the tree, of its height, and of its spreading branches. Fred spoke of the roots, some of which he had seen a long distance from the foot of the tree. Mary described the branches, and drew upon the blackboard the shape of a leaf she had brought with her. Martha said that she had been specially interested in a bird's nest that she had discovered on one of the branches, and gave an interesting account of the birds she had seen carrying straws into the tree.

LESSON VII.

Conversation Exercise.

1. Is there a large tree near your school-house? What kind of tree is it? Has it spreading branches?

2. Have you ever seen any of its roots? How far from the foot of the tree do you think they reach? Why must such a tree have large and long roots?

3. What kind of bark on the tree? Are the lowest branches very near the ground? Can you draw the shape of one of the leaves on the blackboard?

4. Have you ever seen a bird's nest in the tree? Where was the nest? Of what was it made? Did you see the birds building it? What kind of birds were they?

To the Teacher. — These questions are only suggestions. They must be modified to suit different circumstances. Be sure that leaves and twigs are brought into the school-house, described, and drawn.

LESSON VIII.

Composition.

Write a composition about a large tree near your own school-house. Let it be a story in which you speak of a teacher who sent four of her pupils to examine the tree. Give the names of the pupils and tell what each one said after having visited the tree. How many paragraphs will you have in your composition? Why?

LESSON IX.

Review.

First *oral* and then *written*.

In the following sentences, use plural nouns instead of the nouns in italics, and make such other changes as are necessary:

1. The *bird* carries straws in its *mouth* to build its nest.
2. It builds its *nest* in a tall tree.
3. There is a *nest* in a *tree* near our house.
4. There is a blue *egg* in this nest.
5. The *egg* has black spots on it.
6. A little *boy* knows where the *bird* has its *nest*.
7. Do you think this *boy* will harm the *nest?* Not he!
8. He watched the *bird* while it was building its *nest*.
9. He likes to hear it sing its sweet *song*.
10. The *boy* thinks a *bird* has as good a right to live and be happy as a *boy* has.
11. He calls any *boy* who will harm a bird's *nest* a *coward* and a *bully*.

LESSON X.

Pronounce the following words as marked:

for băde'	ġĕn'tle man	ī de'a
ĕn'ġĭne	hăl lōō'	in stĕad'
drowned	heīght	ĭ tăl'ics
drown'ing	ho rī'zon	noth'ing (o=ŭ)

After studying the foregoing words, copy them upon your slate, then close your book and mark each word to denote its proper pronunciation.

Use each word in an oral sentence.

To the Teacher.—It will be profitable to review frequently the pronunciation of the foregoing and similar lists of words.

LESSON XI.

Story from a Picture.

Suggestions.

1. Name of boy — city — had been at school — after school.
2. Appearance of street.
3. Old lady — poor — bundle — hard work.
4. What the boy did.
5. Kindness to the poor — respect for age.

LESSON XII.

Write a story about "A Noble Boy," following the suggestions given in Lesson XI.

LESSON XIII.

Homonyms.

Words that have exactly the same sound but different spellings are called hŏm'-o-nўms as, *air*, *heir*; *tail*, *tale*. Select the homonyms in the following sentences:

1. There are some birds near their nest in that tree.
2. Two dinners are too many for one day.
3. The boys rode their ponies on the road to Boston.

Copy the following words, and after each write its homonym:

hear	right	bear ....
no	would	blue ....
nose	not	course ....
meet ...	dear	four ....

Oral.

1. Use in a sentence each of the words in the printed list.
2. Show that you know the meaning of the words in your own list by using them in sentences.

LESSON XIV.

Abbreviations.

A. D., *In the Year of our Lord.*
Amt., *Amount.*
B. C., *Before Christ.*
Co., *Company.*
C. O. D., *Collect on Delivery.*
Cr., *Credit, Creditor.*

D. C., *District of Columbia.*
Dr., *Debtor.*
Gov., *Governor.*
Pres., *President.*
R. R., *Railroad.*
U. S. A., *United States of America.*

1. Copy the foregoing abbreviations, then close your book and write the proper word or words after each.

2. Make a list of the words or phrases to be abbreviated, and then write the proper abbreviation after each.
3. What is the meaning of each of these dates, 50 B. C., 50 A. D.?
4. How many years from 50 A. D. to the present time?
5. Explain how each of the other abbreviations might be used.

LESSON XV.

Information Exercise.

To the Teacher.—Before dictating any part of the information exercise below, give an *observation* exercise on the sponge. Require the pupils to examine a sponge very carefully, under your direction, and to make notes of their observations.

THE SPONGE.

A sponge when alive is a colony of animals. At first, an object appears like a small yellow egg swimming in the water. This contains the real eggs. It fastens itself to some hard substance. Here the tiny animals increase in numbers until they look like a mass of jelly. The larger openings in the sides are inlets for food to the colony.

Look at the sponge on your desk. The jelly is all gone. It is a skeleton of the mass. Observe the openings in the sides. These are canals to carry the food to all parts of the mass. Very tiny animals and plants in the water furnish the sponge with food. There are little canals to carry the food to all parts of the body. What it does not need, is thrown out of the large holes on top. Divers go down to the bed of the ocean to get sponges. The sponges are put into large tanks of shallow water. There they decay, the jelly falling off. The skeleton is left. This is washed and dried in the sun. The best sponges are found in the Mediterranean Sea.

Note.—The information exercise on "The Sponge" should be divided into a number of *dictation* exercises for the pupils.

LESSON XVI.

Sponges.

Questions to be answered in complete sentences from the foregoing information lesson.

1. What is the sponge?
2. What does a sponge look like in its earliest stages?
3. Where does the sponge live?
4. To what does it fasten itself?
5. What is its food?
6. Where are its mouths?
7. Of what use are the large holes on top?
8. How do divers get sponges?
9. What is done to a sponge before we can use it?
10. To what sea would you go to get the best sponges?

To the Teacher. — In this lesson require pupils to describe sponges which they have, and to give connected oral accounts of their growth.

LESSON XVII.

Composition.

Write all that you have learned about the sponge. Remember directions and cautions already given you in regard to writing.

LESSON XVIII.

Another Use for the Apostrophe.

Sometimes a letter is omitted in writing a word, or two words are joined together with one or more letters omitted. The new words thus formed are called *contractions;* as, *o'er, don't.*

In contractions the apostrophe is used in place of omitted letters.

1. Copy the following contractions, and write after each the word or words in full:

it's	I'll	had n't ....
can 't	won't	I'm ....
I've	o'er	would n't ....
do n't	did n't	he 'll ....
does n't	there 's	't was ....
we 'll	e'er	ma'am ....

2. Name the letter or letters omitted in each contraction.

3. What difference can you see between contractions and abbreviations?

Note. — Contractions should be used sparingly, but correctly if used at all.

LESSON XIX.

Study and commit to memory the following poem:

THE THREE BELLS.

1. Beneath the low-hung night-cloud
    That raked her splintering mast,
   The good ship settled slowly,
    The cruel leak gained fast.

2. Over the awful ocean
    Her signal guns pealed out.
   Dear God! was that thy answer
    From the horror round about?

3. A voice came down the wild wind,
    "Ho! ship ahoy!" its cry:
   "Our stout Three Bells of Glasgow
    Shall lay till daylight by."

LANGUAGE EXERCISES. 53

4. Hour after hour crept slowly,
   Yet on the heaving swells
   Tossed up and down the ship-lights,
   The lights of The Three Bells.

5. And ship to ship made signals,
   Man answered back to man,
   While oft, to cheer and hearten,
   The Three Bells nearer ran;

6. And the captain, from her taffrail,
   Sent down his hopeful cry:
   "Take heart! hold on!" he shouted,
   "The Three Bells shall lay by!"

7. All night, across the waters
   The tossing lights shone clear;
   All night from reeling taffrail
   The Three Bells sent her cheer.

8. And when the dreary watches
   Of storm and darkness passed,
   Just as the wreck lurched under,
   All souls were saved at last.

9. Sail on, Three Bells, forever,
   In grateful memory sail!
   Ring on, Three Bells of rescue,
   Above the wave and gale!

10. Type of the Love eternal,
    Repeat the Master's cry,
    As tossing through our darkness
    The lights of God draw nigh.
                    JOHN G. WHITTIER.

LESSON XX.

Oral Exercise.

1. How many ships are spoken of in the poem, "The Three Bells"? Tell something about each of them. Describe the night.

2. What are "signal guns"? In the third verse of the second stanza, what does "that" refer to? What does the question mean?

3. Whose voice "came down the wild wind"? What did it say? What is meant by "heaving swells"? Did you ever see any "ship-lights"? What are they?

4. Give the meaning of the fifth stanza. Of the sixth. What is a "taffrail"? Why does the poet say "reeling taffrail"? What is meant by "sent her cheer"?

5. What time is referred to in the eighth stanza? What happened then? What is meant by "lurched under"?

6. Why does the poet say "Sail on forever"? Why does he say "Three Bells of rescue"? What is meant by "type"? by "Love eternal"? Who is the "Master"? What does the last stanza mean?

To the Teacher. — Tell the children about Mr. Whittier, and at suitable times read "Barefoot Boy," "Barbara Frietchie," and other poems that they can understand and enjoy.

LESSON XXI.

Composition.

Write the story of "The Three Bells."

CHAPTER FIVE.

LESSON I.

Letter-Writing.

A LETTER is a kind of composition, and it should always be carefully written. The *form* of a letter is of great importance, especially as regards the first and the last part of it.

A letter is made up of four parts: the *heading*, the *salutation*, the *body of the letter*, and the *conclusion*. Another matter of great importance is the *address* on the envelope, or the *superscription*.

Notice carefully the arrangement, the capital letters, and marks of punctuation in the following letter, and then copy it.

HEADING.

Waltham, Mass., Dec. 11, 1888.

SALUTATION.

My dear Mother,

BODY OF LETTER.

I arrived safe and on time. The journey did not seem long, as I was much interested in watching the strange country through which we passed.

LANGUAGE EXERCISES.

Aunt Amy met me at the station, and in a few minutes we were chatting merrily over a good warm supper.

CONCLUSION.

Your loving daughter,
Jennie.

LESSON II.

Headings.

The heading of a letter should indicate the place where, and the time when, the letter was written. When answering a letter, a person looks to the heading to see how to direct his answer.

In the letter in Lesson I., *Waltham, Mass.*, tells where the letter was written, and *Dec. 11, 1888*, tells when it was written. If this letter had been written in a large city, the *number and street* should also have been given in the heading.

Study carefully the arrangement, capitals, and punctuation of the following headings:

Dictation Exercise.

Scranton, R. I., Nov. 7, 1885.

Winchester, Middlesex Co., Mass.,
Tuesday, March 13, 1888.

Cook Co. Normal School,
Englewood, Illinois,
April 15, 1881.

149 Wabash Ave., Chicago, Ill.
March 21, 1887.

LESSON III.

Oral Exercise.

1. Of what should the *heading* of a letter consist?
2. What is the *use* of the heading?
3. What items should be contained in the heading of a letter which is written in a village?
4. What additional items should be contained in the heading of a letter written in a large city? Why?
5. Tell what marks of punctuation you would use in the heading.

Written Exercise.

Write the following *headings*, taking care to arrange and punctuate them correctly:

1. New York, Auburn, Jan. 4, 1880.
2. June 16, 1879, Mass., Boston, 47 Exeter St.
3. Chicago, Ill., Palmer House, 1875, April 14.
4. Columbia, S. C., April 19, 1888, Laurel St., No. 84.
5. What heading would you use, if writing a letter from your own home?

LESSON IV.

The Salutation.

The *salutation* is the term of politeness, respect, or affection, with which we introduce a letter.

In letters to dear friends the following salutations are used:

My dear Mother.   Dear Uncle.
My dear Henry.   Dear Miss Johnson, etc.

Copy the following forms and notice carefully the position, capitals, and punctuation of the *headings* and *salutations:*

     Charleston, S. C., Aug. 8, 1888.
My dear Mother,
 I am very glad to hear, etc.

     Englewood, Ill., April 15, 1888.
Dear Uncle,
 My father has been very sick, etc.

     Jacksonville, Fla., Sept. 12, 1888.
Dear Miss Johnson,
 You must have heard, etc.

In letters to strangers or to very slight acquaintances, the following forms of salutation are used:

Mr. Robert James,   Mrs. Addison Ray,
 Dear Sir,   Dear Madam,
Jerome Bates, Esq.,   Miss Emma James,
 Dear Sir,   Dear Madam,

The *salutation* should in general be followed by a

comma as in the examples given; or, if the letter begins on the same line, by a comma and a dash; as,

Rev. Thos. H. Wilson,
Dear Sir,—I am pleased to learn, etc.

To the Teacher.—Require these salutations to be copied and afterwards written from dictation.

LESSON V.

Oral Exercise.

What would be the *salutation*, if you were writing a letter to your mother? father? brother? sister? a schoolmate? a friend? a gentleman whom you had met only once or twice? an unmarried lady who is an intimate friend? a married lady who is a slight acquaintance?

Written Exercise.

1. Write the *heading* and *salutation* of a letter to your mother, from Albany, March 7, 1880.
2. To your brother, from Scranton, Pa., April 4, 1879.
3. To a gentleman and near friend, from Chicago, Ill., 486 Wabash Avenue, Jan. 8, 1875.
4. To your teacher, from your own home to-day.
5. To a schoolmate, from Washington, D. C., 54 H St., Jan. 1, 1884.

To the Teacher.—In an oral exercise to precede the written, require exact *descriptions* of capitals, punctuation, and position.

LESSON VI.

The Conclusion.

The *conclusion* of a letter is that which is added after the body of the letter is finished. It consists of the *complimentary close*, and of the *signature*.

LANGUAGE EXERCISES.

The *complimentary close*, consisting of words of respect or affection, is written on the line below the body of the letter. If long, it may occupy two, or even more, lines.

The *signature* is written on the line next below the *complimentary close*.

Be careful that neither is crowded too far to the right-hand edge of the paper.

Dictation Exercise.

CONCLUSIONS.

Your loving daughter,
    Jennie.

Yours respectfully,
    M. J. Cherrington.

Yours truly,
    Robert Richmond.

Your affectionate nephew,
    James Bradley.

Sincerely your friend,
    Allen Thornton.

LESSON VII.

Oral Review.

1. What does the *conclusion* of a letter include?
2. What is meant by the *complimentary close?* by the *signature?* by the *salutation?*
3. What would be a proper *complimentary close* of a letter to your father? mother? brother? sister? friend?
4. Where should the *signature* be written? the *salutation?*
5. What items should appear in the *heading* of a letter?
6. How should the heading be punctuated?
7. What is the difference between the heading of a letter written in a village and one written in a city?
8. Describe the *salutation* and the *conclusion* of a letter written to your father, giving capitals and punctuation.
9. Describe the *exact position* of the different parts of the heading, the address, and the conclusion.

To the Teacher. — The forms of letters cannot be too carefully impressed. In addition to the foregoing, call for a similar arrangement of many different headings, addresses, and conclusions, being careful that they occupy the same relative positions.

LESSON VIII.

A Letter.

Write a letter of three paragraphs to your teacher about the events of yesterday. Show that you can write a correct heading, salutation, and conclusion.

LESSON IX.

The Envelope.

Turn to Lesson I., and you will find a letter from Jennie to her mother. Before this letter is *posted*, it must be folded and placed in an envelope, which should be properly directed. We will suppose that Jennie's father is living in Greytown, Pa., and that his name is Philip C. Murray. She would direct the letter as follows:—

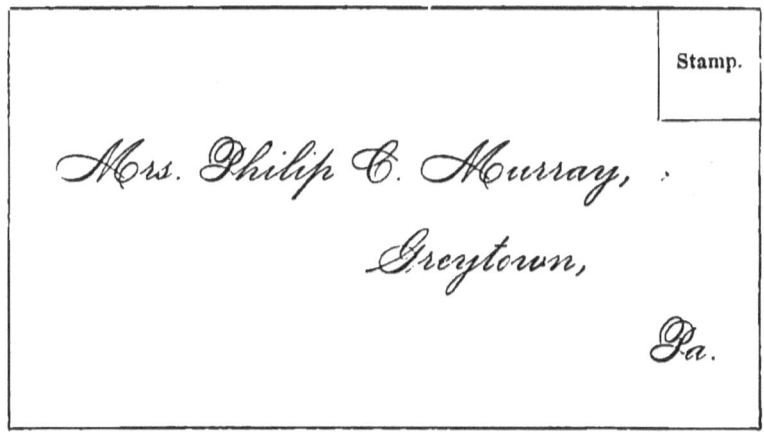

If Mrs. Murray's residence were in a large city like Philadelphia, the street and number should be added to the *address* on the envelope, as follows:—

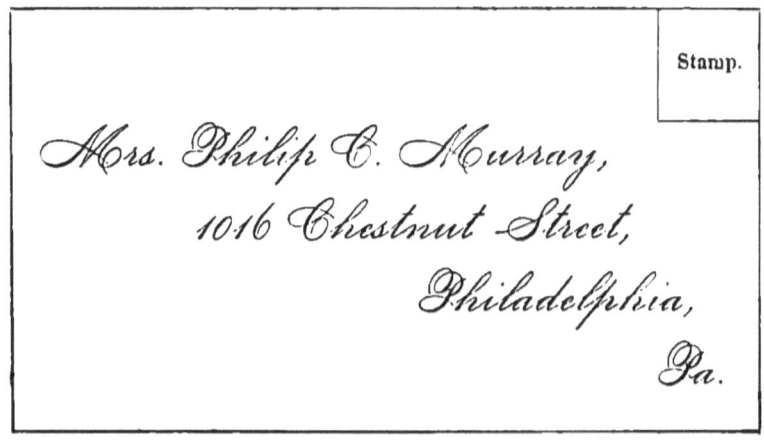

The width of an envelope is usually a very little more than one half the length.

Written Exercise.

Draw five rectangles representing five envelopes. Direct them to the following persons:

1. To your teacher at her own home.
2. To your father or mother.
3. To Mrs. Jas. R. Munroe, who resides at 47 High St., Providence, R. I.
4. To Mr. C. R. Stetson, who is a clergyman living in Bloomington, Ill.
5. To George E. Davis, at 1896 Lake St., Chicago, Ill.

LESSON X.

A Letter.

John Harrison, of San Francisco, writes to his friend Walter Manning, of Chicago, March 1, 1887.

The following is an analysis of his letter. Make as many paragraphs as there are topics.

Analysis.

1. The weather for the past month. 2. His father has been very sick. 3. He has a small garden of his own, — tells what he has planted. 4. He asks Walter to visit him, and describes the route.

Write the letter in full. Draw and direct the envelope.

To the Teacher. — In this grade, a conversation lesson upon the letter-topics should always precede an exercise in letter-writing, and should include a careful consideration of the forms and punctuation of headings, salutations, and conclusions.

64 LANGUAGE EXERCISES.

LESSON XI.

Story from a Picture.

ONE CHRISTMAS.

Suggestions.

1. The names of the children and their home.
2. Christmas-time in their home.
3. People to whom Christmas brings little happiness.
4. How the children came to think of others.
5. Their visit, what they found, and what they did.
6. Why we should remember the poor, especially at Christmas-time.

To the Teacher. — A well-directed conversation lesson should precede any attempt at writing from a picture.

LANGUAGE EXERCISES. 65

LESSON XII.

Homonyms.

Copy the following words, and place after each another word having exactly the same sound but different spelling.

great	pane	threw ....
flour	rode	whole ....
pair	sail	stairs ....
pale	steal	tail ....

Oral Exercise.

1. Use in a sentence each word of the foregoing list.
2. Use in a sentence each word that you have supplied.
3. Review the lesson on homonyms in Chapter Four.

LESSON XIII.

Information Exercise.

To the Teacher.—Pieces of coral should be brought into the class and examined. Pupils should be encouraged to gather information from every available source.

CORAL.

Coral is made by an animal called a polyp. Its home is chiefly in the warm, clear waters of the sea. In form it is like a flower. The body is the stem, and at the top is a disk with feathery feelers round it. At the middle of the disk is the mouth, and below this is a cavity which serves for a stomach. With these feelers round the top, the polyp can catch any small living thing that comes near; for these organs can grasp and paralyze the prey, and so pass it to the mouth to be swallowed. On the side of the stem or body of the polyp a bud will start. This will grow to a polyp and will retain its place united to the parent. From the new animal another bud will start and grow to a polyp, and so on until a coral branch or tree is formed. Should one of these animals lose a part of itself by injury, it will restore the lost part by a new growth. The coral which is brought to us shows the exact form of the inside of the stems, or body, of the polyp, hence it is often called the skeleton of the animal. Though usually very small, these animals make vast deposits; for the southern extremity of the peninsula of Florida rests upon coral.

Topics for Study.

Parts of the coral animal,— where it is found,— kind of water,— food,— how caught. "The builder,"— why so called. — Land that rests upon coral. — Different kinds of coral,— the most beautiful,— where found. — Uses of coral.

LESSON XIV.

Composition.

Write all that you have learned about the coral. Make any use you please of the topics in Lesson XIII.

LESSON XV.

Oral Exercise.

To the Teacher.—The pupils are supposed to have gained all necessary information from some previous exercise. An actual visit to a blacksmith's shop would be the best possible preparation for the lesson. Require the pupils to tell orally all that they know about each of the following topics.

THE BLACKSMITH.

1. Introduction.
   (1) Different kinds of smiths.
   (2) Business of the blacksmith.
2. Materials used.
3. Names of the tools.
4. Uses of the tools.
5. Forge and bellows.
6. The anvil.
7. Kinds of work done.

LESSON XVI.

Composition.

Write upon each topic in Lesson XV., dividing your work into seven paragraphs.

LESSON XVII.

Oral Exercise.

Pronounce the following words according to the marking:

läugh'ter	prŏb'a bly	shriēked
lēi'șure	rē'al ly	sĭt'ting
nĕsts	rĕg'ū lar	sĭxth
pīet'ūre	rĭ dĭc'ū loŭs	stămped

1. In the first word what sound has *gh*?
2. Give the vowel sound in each accented syllable.
3. Give the vowel sound in each monosyllable.
4. Give all the vowel sounds in the polysyllable.
5. Pronounce the two shortest words very distinctly.
6. Show that you know the meaning of each word by using it in a sentence.

LESSON XVIII.

A Letter.

Suppose a letter to have been written by Walter Manning, of Chicago, Ill., in reply to John Harrison, of San Francisco, Cal. It was dated June 1, 1887.

Suggestions.

Walter is glad to hear from John. Health of himself and family. Has a nice boat, — describes it. Sailing party on the Lake, — no accident except the loss of one or two hats. Would be pleased to visit John, — gives reason why he cannot do so this summer.

Write the letter in full. Draw and direct the envelope.

LESSON XIX.

Reproduction.

Read the following incident once or twice carefully, and write the thoughts in your own words without referring to the book. Divide your story into three paragraphs.

Learn the saying of Horace Mann, and write it word for word at the end of your story. Be sure that you know exactly what the saying means and never forget it.

THE FORCE OF HABIT.

There was once a horse that used to pull around a sweep which lifted dirt from the depths of the earth. He was kept at the business for nearly twenty years, until he became old, blind, and too stiff in the joints for further use. So he was turned into a pasture, or left to crop the grass without any one to disturb or bother him.

The funny thing about the old horse was that every morning, after grazing awhile, he would start on a tramp, going round and round in a circle, just as he had been accustomed to do for so many years. He would keep it up for hours, and people often stopped to look and wonder what had got into the head of the venerable animal to make him walk around in such a solemn way when there was no earthly need of it. It was the force of habit.

The boy who forms bad or good habits in his youth will be led by them when he becomes old, and will be miserable or happy accordingly. — SELECTED.

Habit is a cable, — we weave a thread of it each day, and at last we cannot break it. — HORACE MANN.

To the Teacher. — The "Stories for Reproduction" in this book are given merely as suggestions as to the *kind* to be chosen, and the *manner* of treatment. Let the story be read by the pupils once or twice, and then be made the subject of conversation. An oral reproduction should usually follow the conversation exercise and precede the written work.

LESSON XX.

Study and commit to memory the following poem:

THE FIRST SNOW-FALL.

1. The snow had begun in the gloaming,
    And busily all the night
  Had been heaping field and highway
    With a silence deep and white.

2. Every pine and fir and hemlock
    Wore ermine too dear for an earl,
  And the poorest twig on the elm-tree
    Was ridged inch deep with pearl.

   .   .   .   .   .   .

3. I stood and watched by the window
    The noiseless work of the sky,
  And the sudden flurries of snow-birds,
    Like brown leaves whirling by.

4. I thought of a mound in sweet Auburn
    Where a little headstone stood;
  How the flakes were folding it gently,
    As did robins the babes in the wood.

5. Up spoke our own little Mabel,
    Saying, "Father, who makes it snow?"
  And I told of the good All-Father
    Who cares for us here below.

   .   .   .   .   .   .

6. Then, with eyes that saw not, I kissed her;
    And she, kissing back, could not know
  That *my* kiss was given to her sister,
    Folded close under deepening snow.

JAMES RUSSELL LOWELL.

LANGUAGE EXERCISES.

LESSON XXI.

Oral Exercise.

1. At what time in the day did it begin to snow? How do you know? At what time was Mr. Lowell speaking? How did he know that the snow had been busy all the night? What is the meaning of the last verse in the first stanza?

2. What is ermine? What is its color? Why should it be costly? What is an earl? What is the meaning of the last verse in the second stanza? Describe the picture that this stanza brings to your mind.

3. What two things was the poet watching from his window? What was he thinking about? Where is "Sweet Auburn"? Tell the story of "The Babes in the Wood."

4. Who was watching the snow with the poet? What is meant by "All-Father"? By "eyes that saw not"? Tell the meaning of the sixth stanza.

LESSON XXII.

Written Exercise.

1. Write in your own words the meaning of the poem.

To the Teacher. — From time to time read with the children, and talk about any or all of the poems here named: — "The Heritage," "The Courtin'," "Aladdin," "The Singing Leaves," "The Finding of the Lyre," "Without and Within," "The Beggar," "The Changeling." See page 223.

It may be necessary to assign some of these poems to a higher grade.

PART II.

TO TEACHERS.

THE value of committing to memory choice selections of prose or poetry as a means of language-training can hardly be over-estimated. It would be difficult to find a single individual, noted as a writer or speaker, whose success cannot be traced directly to the habit, acquired when young, of memorizing favorite extracts from the writings of famous authors.

The best talkers are likely to be those who associate with the best talkers; the best writers those who are most familiar with the best literature. The great poets know the poems of other great poets by heart; thoughtful men are always studying the writings of thoughtful men.

John Bright could repeat from memory whole poems of favorite authors, and his wonderful power over the English language could, without doubt, be traced to his familiarity with the best writers and speakers of his own time.

A study of the lives of the great scholars of America would reveal the fact that much of their success in the use of the English language has come from the habit of committing to memory whatever seemed to them worthy of their time and study.

Teachers can do no better service for their pupils than to make the study of choice selections from the writings of our best authors a prominent part of the language-training of the school.

CHAPTER SIX.

LESSON I.

Quotations.

IN speaking or writing, we frequently wish to tell what another person has said: as, Yesterday, Joseph Williams told me that he was too young to enter the High School. In this case we simply express in our own words what Joseph Williams said. Such expressions are called *indirect quotations*.

An indirect quotation is the thought of another expressed in our own words.

It often happens that we wish to express the thought of another in his own words: as, Yesterday, I heard Joseph Williams say, "I am too young to enter the High School." Such expressions are called *direct quotations*, and, in writing, are enclosed by quotation marks (" ").

Titles of books, pictures, poems, or newspapers, assumed names of writers, etc., are usually written with quotation marks: as, "Our Old Home"; the "Sistine Madonna"; "Gray's Elegy"; the "New York Herald"; "Oliver Optic" (William T. Adams).

A direct quotation is the thought of another expressed in his own words.

A comma usually precedes a direct quotation that does not stand at the beginning of a sentence. Punctuation marks that belong to a quotation must stand within the quotation marks.

To the Teacher. — Read Lesson I. with the pupils, and then question them carefully as to its meaning. This lesson should be thoroughly understood before Lesson II. is undertaken.

LESSON II.

Dictation Exercise.

1. Pope says, " Virtue alone is happiness below."
2. Our teacher told me that the leaves and flowers would soon be out.
3. " Can't you contrive to be present at our exhibition?" said Lucy.
4. The Bible says that we should honor our fathers and our mothers.
5. A well-known voice echoed from the silent mound, " Hurrah! let them come on to Breed's; the people will teach 'em the law."

Oral.

1. Give a reason for each use of the apostrophe in the dictation exercise.
2. Give reasons for the use of the quotation marks.
3. Which sentences contain *indirect quotations?*
4. Read the *direct quotations.*
5. Change the second indirect quotation to a direct quotation.
6. Change the first direct quotation to an indirect quotation.

LANGUAGE EXERCISES. 75

LESSON III.

Sentence-making.

1. Write five sentences, each containing a direct quotation.
2. Re-write the sentences, changing the direct quotations to indirect.

Model.

Direct quotation. — John replied, "I do not intend to return."
Indirect quotation. — John replied that he did not intend to return.

1. Write or select five sentences, using the apostrophe to show possession.
2. Write or select five sentences, using the apostrophe in contractions.

LESSON IV.

A Fable.

A Hare once made fun of a Tortoise. "What a slow way you have!" he said. "How you creep along!"

"Do I?" said the Tortoise. "Try a race with me, and I will beat you."

"You only say that for fun," said the Hare. "But come! I will race with you. Who will mark off the bounds and give the prize?"

"Let us ask the Fox," said the Tortoise.

The Fox was very wise and fair; so he showed them where they were to start, and how far they were to run.

The Tortoise lost no time. She started at once, and jogged straight on. The Hare knew he could come to the end in two or three jumps, so he lay down and took a nap first. By and by he awoke, and then ran fast; but when he came to the end, the Tortoise was already there.

Slow and steady wins the race.

LANGUAGE EXERCISES.

Oral.

1. Are the quotations in this fable direct or indirect?
2. Read the quotations only.
3. Try to tell the story in your own words, using no direct quotations.
4. What is a fable? What does this one teach?
5. Why should the Hare and the Tortoise be selected to illustrate this fable?

Written.

Write the story of the "Hare and the Tortoise" in your own words, and tell what you think it means.

LESSON V.

Verb-forms.

The word *break* suggests *breaks, breaking, broke, broken.*
The word *bite* suggests *bites, biting, bit, bitten.*
The word *eat* suggests *eats, eating, ate, eaten.*
The word *drive* suggests *drives, driving, drove, driven.*

The first three words of each set are used correctly by almost everybody. The last two words of each set cause many errors. The trouble arises from using one for the other.

The *fifth* word in each set is commonly used after one of the following words:—*have, has, had, having, be, is, am, are, was, were, being, been.*

The *fourth* word in each set should *never* be used after one of those words.

1. Construct sentences to show that you can use the last two words of the four sets above correctly.

To the Teacher.—Confine the drill to the parts of the verb that cause errors. Review the lesson frequently.

LESSON VI.
Information Exercise.

WORKER-BEE. QUEEN-BEE. DRONE.

THE HONEY BEE.

There are three kinds of bees in every hive,—females or queens, males, and workers. The males, which are often called drones, do not work. The workers make the wax, with which they build the cells, collect the honey, and feed and protect the young. The males have no stings. Only one full-grown female lives in a hive, and she is called the queen. After she has laid eggs in the cells prepared for them, the workers supply these cells with the pollen of flowers. This is mixed with honey and water, and forms the food of the little white worms that hatch from the eggs. These little worms change into workers, males, or queens. Some of the worms are fed with a richer food than is given to the others, and these become queens. Five days after they are hatched they spin cocoons, and in sixteen days more come out perfect queen-bees. The workers and males have a slower growth.

To the Teacher. — Language exercises based on elementary science lessons presuppose careful observation work on the part of the pupils. It is no part of the work of this book to give elementary science lessons, but rather to suggest how exercises in language may be made from *information* gained from a science lesson.

Topics for Study.

Different kinds of bees, — queen-bees, — drones, — workers. Hives, — honeycomb, — wax, — cells, — eggs, — cocoons. Bee-hunting, — gathering honey.

To the Teacher. — Read to the class, "Bees," by John Burroughs.

LESSON VII.
Words and their Opposites.

1. Write the opposites of the following words:—*before, left, large, fast, long, rough, sweet, brittle.*
2. Write eight sentences, each of which shall contain one of the words above, and its opposite.

Abbreviations.

The following are the abbreviations of names of days and months. Learn them, and write the words for which they stand. Be careful about the name of the middle day of the week and of the shortest month.

Sun.	Thurs.	Feb.	Sept.
Mon.	Fri.	Mar.	Oct.
Tues.	Sat.	Apr.	Nov.
Wed.	Jan.	Aug.	Dec.

May, June, and July should never be abbreviated.

LESSON VIII.
Synonyms.

Synonyms are words which have the same or similar meanings: as, *droll, comical; forgive, pardon.*

In the following sentence, the word *own* may be used instead of *possess* and the meaning will be the same: I should like to *possess* a horse and carriage. The words *possess* and *own* are synonyms.

From the following list, select a synonym for each word in the columns below:—*port, gift, share, pursue, empty, hide, house, brave, crack, careless, fright, polite.* Example: *gift, present; port, harbor,* etc.

courteous	present	vacant	conceal
harbor	follow	heedless	alarm
portion	fearless	fracture	residence

Construct five sentences which shall contain five of the words in the first list, used correctly.

Substitute for the words taken from the first list the synonyms taken from the second.

Which of the words do you prefer to use in your sentences?

Which synonyms seem to have the same meaning?

Example.

1. The teacher made me a *gift* of a beautiful book.
2. The teacher made me a *present* of a beautiful book.

To the Teacher. — The object of this exercise is to teach pupils that while synonyms have *similar* meanings, the meanings are not always the *same.*

LESSON IX.

A Letter.

FRED TO HIS AUNT MARY.

Cold weather .... a severe snow-storm .... streets blocked .... no school. Made a snow man last week .... tells how .... size .... eyes .... nose .... mouth .... arms .... Warm weather came on .... snow man disappeared.

Write Fred's letter in full.

Exercise.

1. When and where is your letter dated?
2. What is the "address"?
3. What mark of punctuation follows the "address"?
4. What capital letters are used in the letter because they begin proper names?
5. What capital letters are used because they begin sentences?

6. What is the *conclusion* of your letter?

7. What marks of punctuation besides periods have you used in your letter? Why?

LESSON X.

Homonyms.

Write after each of the following words its homonym:

not	eight	hare ....
there	brake	lane ....
week	lief	grown ....
too	knead	heel ....

1. Use in sentences the words in the printed list.

2. Use in sentences the homonyms that you have supplied.

LESSON XI.

Dictation Exercise.

1. "Maud Muller" is the name of a poem written by John G. Whittier.

2. Do you know who wrote "The Old Clock on the Stairs"?

3. Dr. O. W. Holmes wrote "The Autocrat of the Breakfast Table."

4. Jennie took, as the title of her composition, "One Christmas." "How we spent Vacation" would be an easy subject to write about.

5. Behind the cloud the starlight lurks,
   Through showers the sunbeams fall;
  For God, who loveth all his works,
   Has left his hope with all.
  JOHN G. WHITTIER.

LANGUAGE EXERCISES. 81

LESSON XII.

A Picture-Study.
First *oral* and then *written*.

Suggestions.

1. Describe the picture,—that is, tell exactly what you see in it.
2. Describe the inside of the house as you imagine it, and the family of which you see a part.
3. Give a history of the family or a story suggested by the picture.

To the Teacher. — Any or all of the foregoing suggestions may be followed. Give time for the preparatory exercises, even if they occupy two or three lessons.

LESSON XIII.

1. Pronounce the following words according to the marking:

kēpt	sĕv'en	tăs'sĕl
läun'dry	swĕpt	tōw'ard
pär tĭc'ū lar	slĕpt	tī'ny
sŭp pōse'	dȧnç'ing	tŏss'ing

2. Show clearly the meaning of each word by using it in a sentence.

3. Review all the exercises in pronunciation that precede this one.

LESSON XIV.

A Letter.

AUNT MARY TO FRED.

Was glad to receive a letter from him .... surprised to find that he could write so well .... thinks he must be a big boy and a good scholar. Tells him of a great snow-storm some years ago .... was obliged to walk two miles through the snow .... thinks she looked like a snow woman. She is glad that Fred is enjoying the winter.

Write Aunt Mary's letter in full.

LESSON XV.

Words often Misused.

Real for very.

Real and *very* have meanings quite unlike. The following sentence shows the correct use of the words:

Mrs. Sharp wears a *real* diamond, and she is *very* proud of it.

Of course, if *real* may be used for *very*, then *very* may be used for *real*, and we shall have *very diamonds* and *real proud*, both of which are wrong.

Don't for doesn't.

Write, in sentences, the words for which these contractions stand, beginning as follows:

You do not ....   Charles does not ....   I do not ....
He does ....   The boys ....   The boy .... etc.

Substitute the contractions in your sentences, and you will see their proper use.

Guess for think.

The following sentences show the correct use of *guess* and *think*:

If your hand is closed I may *guess* what is in it, or if I am blindfolded I may *guess* who touched me. If the clouds look dark I *think* it will rain, or it is so cold that I *think* there will be frost to-night.

Complete the following sentences:

.... what is in my pocket. Shall I be late at school? I .... you will, as it is almost nine. How tall am I? I .... you are four feet ten inches.

Have got for have or has.

Have got means *have obtained*. *Have* when used alone means *own* or *have* in *possession*.

We need to use *have got* or *has got* very rarely. We use *have* and *has* frequently.

To the Teacher. — Call for much practice in the correct use of the foregoing words, and frequently review them.

LESSON XVI.

Reproduction.

To the Teacher.—Read carefully to the pupils Whittier's poem, "Barbara Frietchie." Encourage conversation about the poem, and explain what is necessary to a fair understanding of it. Then have the story written as a composition. Be sure that the poem and the poet are associated.

LESSON XVII.

Two or more statements may be combined into one sentence, as follows:

Model.

1. Jessie Brown found a diamond ring.
  She was on her way to school.
  The ring had been dropped into the mud.

Combined.

On her way to school, Jessie Brown found a diamond ring which had been dropped into the mud.

Combine each of the following groups of sentences into one:

2. Baby Maud has fully recovered her health.
  She has been very sick.
3. Our school-house has been rebuilt.
  It was burned down.
  It is on the same site.
4. The birds will return in the Spring.
  They go south every Autumn.
5. Boston is the largest city in New England.
  It is the capital of Massachusetts.
  It is the metropolis of Massachusetts.
6. President Lincoln was shot by John Wilkes Booth.
  He was in a theater at Washington.
  He died the next day.

Write two sentences, similar to those above, that may be combined into one.

Write three sentences that may be combined into one.

LESSON XVIII.

Information Exercise.

THE HONEY-BEE (Continued).

When the little queens are full-grown, the old queen tries to kill them, for she is jealous and wants to reign alone. Either they must be destroyed or she must leave the hive with a part of the bees, to make another home. But the workers keep watch, and do not let her come near the young queens until they are sure she doesn't mean to leave the hive. In that case, she is allowed to sting and kill all the young females, or queens. If, however, she flies off, followed by many of the bees, a young queen is set free. This queen usually departs with another swarm, as it is called, and the next one will do the same if the hive is still too large.

When a young queen refuses to leave the hive, she fights with the remaining queens, and the one that comes off victorious becomes queen and sole mistress of the hive.

Conversation Exercise.

1. Is the queen-bee a good mother?
2. Which bees may be called protectors? Why?
3. What is meant by swarming?
4. What happens when the old queen leaves the hive?
5. Who finally becomes queen of the old hive?

LESSON XIX.

Composition.

Review very carefully Lessons VI. and XVIII. and write what you have learned about the honey-bee. First, make your notes, and determine the number of paragraphs in your composition.

Any information you have gained from observation or from other books should be used to make your account of the honey-bee more complete.

LESSON XX.

Study and commit to memory the following poem:

THE CHILDREN'S HOUR.

1. Between the dark and the daylight,
    When the night is beginning to lower,
    Comes a pause in the day's occupations,
    That is known as the Children's Hour.

2. I hear in the chamber above me
    The patter of little feet,
    The sound of a door that is opened,
    And voices soft and sweet.

3. From my study I see in the lamp-light,
    Descending the broad hall stair,
    Grave Alice, and laughing Allegra,
    And Edith with golden hair.

4. A whisper, and then a silence:
    Yet I know by their merry eyes
    They are plotting and planning together
    To take me by surprise.

5. A sudden rush from the stairway,
    A sudden raid from the hall!
    By three doors left unguarded
    They enter my castle wall!

6. They climb up into my turret
    O'er the arms and back of my chair;
    If I try to escape, they surround me;
    They seem to be everywhere.

7. They almost devour me with kisses,
    Their arms about me entwine,
    Till I think of the Bishop of Bingen
    In his Mouse-Tower on the Rhine!

LANGUAGE EXERCISES. 87

8. Do you think, O blue-eyed banditti,
Because you have scaled the wall,
Such an old mustache as I am
Is not a match for you all!

9. I have you fast in my fortress,
And will not let you depart,
But put you down into the dungeon
In the round-tower of my heart.

10. And there will I keep you forever,
Yes, forever and a day,
Till the walls shall crumble to ruin,
And molder in dust away!

HENRY W. LONGFELLOW.

LESSON XXI.

Analysis of Poem.

To the Teacher.—Question the children closely as to the meaning of the poem. Lead them to see a picture of Longfellow's home life. Speak of his love for children, the proof of which is in the poems which he has written for them and about them.

LESSON XXII.

Composition.

Write a description of a twilight scene in Mr. Longfellow's home, as you can imagine it from studying "The Children's Hour." Try to picture the house, and suppose Mr. Longfellow to have been writing some poem which you have read.

To the Teacher.—At different times read with your pupils, and talk with them about any or all of the following poems: "Paul Revere's Ride," "Wreck of the Hesperus," "Village Blacksmith," "Old Clock on the Stairs," "My Lost Youth," "The Cumberland," "Reaper and Flowers," "Sandalphon," "Weariness." See page 223.

CHAPTER SEVEN.

LESSON I.

Conversation Exercise.

COLD COUNTRIES.

1. Describe the foregoing picture, telling about every kind of object represented.

2. Find out all you can from your Geography and other books about the coldest countries, their direction from us, the kind of people and the animals that live there, how the people live, their houses, food, and occupations.

To the Teacher. — Teachers will find in geography an abundance of material for language lessons. The exercises in this and succeeding chapters are very simple, but they furnish opportunities for pupils to use language intelligently in connection with subjects made familiar through their daily school lessons. Teachers can easily multiply such exercises, and adjust the difficulties to the ability of the class.

LESSON II.

Conversation Exercise.

COLD COUNTRIES (Continued).

1. Describe the interior of one of the houses, as you imagine it in the evening.
2. Tell about the seasons in these countries, and about day and night.
3. What have you read of explorers who have found out about cold countries?

LESSON III.

Composition.

Arrange topics, and write about cold countries.

LESSON IV.

Sounds of Letters.

The sounds of the vowels in the words *sir, her, fur,* are exactly alike. They are marked thus: — ĩ, ẽ, ũ.

Place a mark over each vowel in these words: — *thirsty, burning, prefer, urgent, term, third.*

In the following words, how many different sounds do you find for *th?* — *thee, thin, thus, thick, with, breath, smooth, broth.* In which words is the sound of *th* vocal?

When *th* has a *vocal* sound it is marked thus: — ₜh. Otherwise it is not marked. In which of the foregoing words should *th* be marked to indicate the pronunciation?

Review.

In the following words, indicate the pronunciation by marking the letters in italics: — c*a*ll, wr*e*n, *c*ell, s*a*fe, m*i*ss,

LANGUAGE EXERCISES.

m*a*rk, *th*is, ri*s*e, rove, c*u*re, *g*ive, trap, *g*em, *a*sk, scene, fife, b*u*lb, st*o*p, r*oo*f, c*u*rve, f*oo*t, m*o*ve, fr*u*it, w*o*lf, st*i*r, term.

LESSON V.

Pronounce the words below according to the marking:

ȧsked	elō̱thȩ̱	erăn' bĕr rẙ
ăt tăcked'	erēēk	eoûr' te oŭs
a' nẙ bŏd y (a=ĕ)	drāin	sûr prī̧e'
ea mĕl' o pärd	dràught (gh=f)	̇gē ŏ̱̇g' ra phẙ

1. Copy the words, and mark them for pronunciation without the aid of the book.
2. Use each word in a sentence.
3. Pronounce the words in all similar preceding lessons.

LESSON VI.

Information Exercise.

THE ANT.

The ant is a very industrious little insect, and a very skillful workman. There are many different kinds of ants. Some of them make their homes above ground, of grass, wheat-stalks, sand, etc., and others burrow in wood or clay, making galleries and chambers.

Among ants there are males, females, and workers, just as among bees. The males and females have wings for a short time. The workers take good care of the eggs, and carry them from one chamber to another, according to the amount of heat desired.

When the little white grubs are hatched, they are as helpless as the bee-grubs, and have to be fed and taken care of until old enough to spin cocoons. At the proper time, the workers cut open these cocoons with their jaws and let the little ants out.

Some species of ants have a strange way of going out in great swarms to capture the eggs and cocoons of other tribes of ants. These they carry to their own colonies to hatch, and then make life-long slaves of them.

Topics for Study.

The ant, an insect, — different kinds, — their homes.
Compare the *ants* and the *bees*.
Duties of the workers, — care of the grubs.
Cocoons. Slave-hunters.

LESSON VII.

Composition.

Arrange notes for a composition on ants, and then write a full account of them.

LESSON VIII.

Oral Exercise.

Who or *which*.

Use *who* or *which* in each of the following sentences:

1. The man .... was here has gone to England.
2. The horse .... was lame is as well as ever.
3. The roads .... were muddy are now very dusty.
4. A boy .... is not kind to his mother cannot be happy.
5. Is that James Morton .... was hurt?
6. There go the cows .... have been sold to the farmer.
7. The bird flew from the cage .... has an open door.

To the Teacher. — Test thoroughly the children's discrimination in the use of the foregoing words, and then ask for the rule. Teach no technical terms.

Written Exercise.

1. Write five statements, in each of which the word *who* is correctly used.
2. Write five similar statements, in each of which the word *which* is correctly used.
3. How can you tell when to use *who*, and when to use *which*?

LESSON IX.

Oral Exercise.

Who or whom.

Use *who* or *whom* in each of the following questions:

1. .... is coming into the house with father?
2. To .... did you give the knife?
3. .... do you see on the platform?
4. With .... were you playing?
5. From .... did you receive your new shoes?
6. .... will come with me to the woods?

Ask questions which the following sentences might answer:

1. I came to school with Mary.
2. Charles bought the apple for the baby.
3. James lent his pencil to his sister.
4. I saw Henry Maple.
5. We did not hear anybody.
6. The baby loves Mamma.
7. Susie is standing by her uncle.

Written Exercise.

1. Write the questions for the foregoing answers.
2. Write five questions of your own, using the word *whom*, and write the answer after each question.

LESSON X.

A Letter.

One day Miss Joyce, a teacher in school No. 34, Jonesville, Ohio, asked her pupils to write a letter to Mr. Longfellow, the poet, at his home in Cambridge, Mass.

To this all the pupils agreed, as they had just finished reading one of Mr. Longfellow's beautiful poems.

Before beginning their letters, Miss Joyce questioned them as to what they intended to write.

One little boy wanted to thank Mr. Longfellow for writing the "Children's Hour." Another suggested that they should ask him if he had any little children or grandchildren of his own; and still another, that they should ask him if he really loved little children, or only said so in his poems. One bright-eyed little girl wanted Mr. Longfellow to tell them something more of Alice, Allegra, and Edith, and whether they really did climb upon his chair and into his lap?

One large boy wanted to know whether the story was true, that General Washington, during the war of the Revolution, lived for a little while in the house which was afterwards Mr. Longfellow's.

Many other suggestions were made by the pupils, who afterwards assisted the teacher in arranging, upon the blackboard, notes from which the letter could be written.

1. You may arrange the notes for this letter to Mr. Longfellow just as you think Miss Joyce arranged them.
2. How many paragraphs will you have in your letter?
3. Write the letter to Mr. Longfellow.
4. Draw and direct the envelope.

To the Teacher.—The details of the plan for letter-writing suggested above, may be varied to suit the circumstances of the class.

LESSON XI.

The Comma.

You have already been required to use the comma in the heading, salutation, and close of letters. Please write a heading, a salutation, and a conclusion, and punctuate them correctly.

Notice the use of the comma in the following sentences:

1. Mother, I cannot tell you what has become of the horse.
2. I cannot tell you what has become of the horse, mother.
3. I cannot tell you, mother, what has become of the horse.

You will see that the word *mother*, which denotes address, is *set off* by commas in each sentence.

1. James, Charles, and Henry gathered apples, pears, and grapes.
2. A kitten likes to run, jump, and play.

In these sentences the comma is used to separate words forming a *series*. Point out the two series in the first sentence. What words form a series in the second sentence?

Copy the following, using the comma where required:

1. Where were you Nellie?
2. Corn wheat oats and rye are called grain.
3. Jamestown Va. June 16 1888.
4. I tried to find you Miss Johnson but I could not.
5. We read write sing and recite at school.
6. Yours sincerely James Graham.
7. John was Washington Irving an American?

LESSON XII.

Homonyms.

Write after each word its homonym:

prey	cent	berry ....
ring	sum	pane ....
forth	bough	peace ....
fare	choir	wrap ....

First *oral* and then *written*.

1. Use in a sentence each word in the printed list.
2. Use each word that you have supplied.
3. Review the lesson on homonyms in Chapter Six.

LESSON XIII.

Reproduction.

To the Teacher.— Read with the children the "Wreck of the Hesperus." For the first lesson, be sure that every part of the poem is well understood, and then require the story to be reproduced orally. For the second lesson, call attention to the direct quotations, and ask to have them changed to indirect quotations in the written reproduction. Be sure that the poem is associated with the poet.

LESSON XIV.

Verb-forms.

First *oral* and then *written*.

Name four other words suggested by each of the following: — *go, give, draw, fly, forget.*

go	goes	going	went	gone
give	....	....	....	....
draw	....	....	....	....
fly	....	....	....	....
forget	....	....	....	....

You will probably write and use the first three words of each set correctly, provided you know how to spell them.

Recollect that *have, has, had, be, is, was, being, been*, should never be used before the *fourth word*.

Use the fourth and fifth words of each set in sentences.

To the Teacher.—Study this lesson with the children, in order to develop from their use the correct forms for the words in the last two columns. Review the different parts of Lesson V., Chapter Six.

LESSON XV.

Information Exercise.

THE BEAVER.

The beaver is found in North America and in the Old World. In the winter, five or six of these animals live together as a family, in a house built in the water, of sticks, mud, and stones. These houses are round on top, and the entrance is under water.

If the stream is too shallow, so that the entrance to the house might be closed in the winter by the ice, the beavers living near first build a dam at some suitable place in the stream. For this purpose, in the latter part of summer, they cut down trees with their sharp teeth, and float the trunks down the stream to the place selected for the dam. These are then sunk to the bottom by means of stones. More trees are then added, until the dam is high enough to answer the purpose of the beavers. These trees, with branches and stones, are afterward firmly plastered together with mud.

The houses are then built in the deep water above the dam. The walls of these houses, or lodges, as they are usually called, are very thick; and as, in winter, the mud of which they are chiefly composed is frozen into a solid mass, the beavers have a safe refuge from all their enemies.

LANGUAGE EXERCISES. 97

Composition.

Read the foregoing account of the beaver, and study carefully the picture. From these two sources you will learn something of the habits of this curious animal. Try to find from other sources something about his size, food, industry, manner of life, and of his use to man. Find out if you can how and in what parts of this country he is trapped. Then prepare notes and write an orderly account of him.

To the Teacher. —Such lessons as the foregoing call upon the teacher to devise means for the children to obtain information other than that contained in the brief account given in this book. The chief source of information will, of course, be books. The general information of the children should be drawn upon, also what they can learn at home, — but all must be supplemented and arranged by the teacher.

LESSON XVI.

Review.

First *oral* and then *written*.

Note carefully how each of the following words is printed: — *horse's, child's, men's, wife's, colts', calves', babies', birds', monkey's, mouse's, kittens', robin's.*

1. Tell whether the words are singular or plural.
2. Tell how each word should be written in the opposite number.
3. Use each word in a written sentence.
4. Re-write each sentence, changing the number of the noun which you were required to use.

LESSON XVII.

A Reply.

Mr. Longfellow replies to the pupils in School No. 34, Jonesville, Ohio.

He tells them how happy their letter made him, and that he really loves children. He describes the good times he has with them on the lawn in front of his house, and the games they play.

He answers all the questions the children had asked him in their letter, and hopes they will find time to write him again. The letter closes with a stanza from his poem, "My Arm-Chair."

Reproduce Mr. Longfellow's letter from the notes above, and add the stanza which you think he selected.

Draw the envelope and direct the letter to some pupil in the school mentioned.

To the Teacher. — From the notes given above, the pupils may prepare others from which they can more easily write their letters.

LANGUAGE EXERCISES.

LESSON XVIII.

Synonyms.

Each word in the following list has one or two synonyms in the columns below: — *get, aid, please, mirth, gay, tell, brave.*

assist	gladness	narrate	joy
procure	merry	obtain	cheerful
gladden	bold	help	daring

Arrange the synonyms in twos or threes as the case may be.

For the words in italics in the following sentences, substitute their synonyms, determine whether the meaning is changed or not, and explain fully.

1. With money one can *get* power, but not love.
2. A boy may do much to *aid* his mother.
3. It will *please* your teacher if you say "Good morning."
4. The monkey caused great *mirth* in school.
5. A *gay* company of girls just went by.
6. The captain likes to *tell* his adventures to the children.
7. A *brave* boy will always tell the truth.
8. The prisoner made a *bold* attempt to escape, and the officer was obliged to *procure* assistance.

To the Teacher. — Select from the Dictionary one hundred common words with their synonyms. Arrange in a blank book one hundred carefully constructed sentences, each containing one of the selected words.

As a class exercise, read the sentences and require each one to be repeated by some pupil who will substitute a synonym for the word taken from the Dictionary.

Example.

Teacher. — I called upon the boy to *assist* me.
Pupil. — I called upon the boy to *help* me.

This may also be made a written exercise, each pupil writing every sentence as it is dictated by the teacher.

LESSON XIX.

Combine the following sentences, as in Lesson XVII., Chapter Six:

1. Frank Day has a beautiful pony.
   The pony was given to Frank last Christmas.
2. Our school had a pleasant time at the picnic.
   The picnic was near a small lake.
   The picnic was held in a grove.
3. Benjamin Harrison is President of the United States.
   Mr. Harrison's home is in Indianapolis, Ind.
4. A noble dog saw a child in the water.
   The dog sprang into the water.
   The dog brought the child safely to shore.
5. London is the largest city in the world.
   London is the capital of England.
   London is situated on the Thames River.
6. George Washington was the first President of the United States.
   George Washington is often called "The Father of his Country."
7. Chicago is situated on Lake Michigan.
   Chicago is the largest city in Illinois.
   Chicago is the greatest grain market in the world.
8. A large part of Illinois consists of prairie land.
   Much of this prairie land is very level.
   The prairie land is fertile.
9. The eastern shores of Massachusetts are washed by Massachusetts Bay.
   Massachusetts is often called "The Old Bay State."

Write two sentences and combine them into one.
Write three sentences and combine them into one.

LESSON XX.

Study and commit to memory the following poem by Phœbe Cary:

NOBODY'S CHILD.

1. Only a newsboy, under the light
    Of the lamp-post plying his trade in vain;
  Men are too busy to stop to-night,
    Hurrying home through the sleet and rain.
  Never since dark a paper sold;
    Where shall he sleep, or how be fed?
  He thinks as he shivers there in the cold,
    While happy children are safe in bed.

2. Is it strange if he turns about
    With angry words, then comes to blows,
  When his little neighbor, just sold out,
    Tossing his pennies, past him goes?
  "Stop!" some one looks at him, sweet and mild,
    And the voice that speaks is a tender one:
  "You should not strike such a little child,
    And you should not use such words, my son."

3. Is it his anger or his fears
    That have hushed his voice and stopped his arm?
  "Don't tremble," these are the words he hears;
    "Do you think that I would do you harm?"
  "It is'nt that," and the hand drops down,
    "I wouldn't care for kicks and blows;
  But nobody ever called me son
    Because I'm nobody's child I s'pose."

4. O men! as ye careless pass along,
    Remember the love that has cared for you;
  And blush for the awful shame and wrong
    Of a world where such a thing could be true!

Think what the child at your knee had been
If thus on life's lonely billows tossed;
And who shall bear the weight of the sin,
If one of these "little ones" be lost?

LESSON XXI.

1. Give the picture in the first four verses in your own words. Give the thought in the second four verses.
2. What is meant by "plying his trade"?
3. You may ask the question in the first half of the second stanza in your own words, and answer it.
4. Describe the person who says "Stop."
5. Describe the two boys as you see them.
6. Answer the first question in the third stanza.
7. Who says "It isn't that," and what does he mean?
8. Give the thought in the last half of the third stanza.
9. What caused such a change in the boy's feelings?
10. In the fourth stanza, why does Miss Cary say "*Remember* the love?" Of what love does she speak?
11. Explain the fifth and sixth verses of the fourth stanza.
12. What answer can you give to the last question?
13. Repeat the story of the poem.

To the Teacher. — There will be no trouble in interesting children in many of the poems of Phœbe Cary. Read with them the following or others that you may select: "Suppose," "Ready," "The Prairie on Fire," "The Leak in the Dike," "Little Gottlieb," "What the Frogs Sing," "Legend of the Northland." See page 223.

CHAPTER EIGHT.

LESSON I.

Conversation Exercise.

WARM COUNTRIES.

1. Examine very carefully the picture at the head of this chapter, describe it and tell what it suggests to you.

2. Learn from your Geographies and from other books all you can about warm countries, their direction from us, the kind of people and the animals that live there, how the people live and dress, their houses, food, and occupations.

3. Contrast the seasons, the day and night, and the vegetation, of very cold countries, with those of very warm countries.

4. Imagine a journey and its difficulties in the hottest part of South America, and tell about your travels.

5. Read books of travel giving accounts of life and adventures in Africa, or in southern Asia. Such books may be found in almost any public or private library in the neighborhood.

LESSON II.

Composition.

Write all that you have learned in Lesson I. about warm countries, following the order of the topics below. Divide your composition into four paragraphs.

1. Wet season; dry season; vegetation.
2. People who live in Central America; in Africa; in India; their food and clothing; houses; business.
3. A journey through some hot country; mode of travel; disagreeable experiences; camping-out.
4. Contrast some hot country with your own, showing why it is pleasanter to live here than there.

LESSON III.

Letter-Writing (*Continued*).

In Chapters Five, Six, and Seven, you have written letters from *notes* or *suggestions* given in the book. Of course, before you can become a good letter-writer, you must be able to write without the help of suggestions made by others.

In this chapter you will be required to depend almost entirely upon yourself; but, after a little practice, you will find that you can write just as good letters as when you received help from your book or from your teacher.

Below are the notes made by a boy who visited his grandfather in Rutland, Vt., in July, 1888. From these notes he wrote a letter to his mother.

Notes.

1. Arrival. 2. Description of journey. 3. Account of farm, cattle, horses, etc. 4. Account of fishing-trip one cloudy day. 5. How I helped grandfather about the farm. 6. A little homesick; shall return next week.

Suppose it to be vacation, and that you are visiting relatives either in the city or country.

Prepare and arrange notes from which a letter addressed to your father may be written.

To the Teacher. — It will be well at first to write on the blackboard such topics as may be suggested by the pupils. Before writing letters from them, pupils should be led to arrange the topics in the best possible order, and to give reasons for the arrangement.

LESSON IV.

Prepare notes from which letters could be written on the following subjects:

1. A visit to the South in summer.
2. A visit to the North in winter.
3. An account of a picnic.
4. A boating excursion, including an account of an accident.

To the Teacher. — The foregoing should be a class exercise, and the notes preserved for future use.

LESSON V.

Words often Mispronounced.

Note carefully the marking of each of the following words, and then pronounce very distinctly:

ăl' mond (*l* is silent).   äunt   mū şē' ŭm
răşp' ber ry (*p* is silent).   brōoch   be nēath'
Ăr' ab   jŭst   hĭs' tō rў
Ăr' a bĭe   jäunt   hu̱r räh'

Use each word in a sentence.

To the Teacher. — Accept for illustration of the meaning of these words nothing but well-constructed, thoughtful sentences. The words in similar preceding lessons should be frequently and distinctly pronounced in two-minute or three-minute exercises.

LESSON VI.

Reproduction.

First *oral* and then *written*.

To the Teacher. — Read with the children Phœbe Cary's poem, "The Leak in the Dike." Before reading the poem, conduct a conversation lesson upon the nature of dikes, and the necessity for their construction in Holland. Before the written reproduction, have notes prepared and copied by the children, or placed on the blackboard.

LESSON VII.

Derivative Words.

You will notice that the word *form* appears in each of the following words:

reform	forming	reformer
inform	formed	information
uniform	formation	deformity

The word *form* is called the *root* of all of the other words because it is the most important part; or it may be said that the other words are derived from the root-word. Hence they are called *derivative words*, or *derivatives*.

Each of the derivative words in the first column is formed by prefixing a syllable to the root-word. The syllables thus used are called *prefixes*.

The derivative words in the second column are made by placing syllables after the root-word. Syllables so used are called *affixes* or *suffixes*.

You may tell how the derivatives in the third column are formed?

Use in a sentence each of the words derived from *form*, to show that you know its meaning.

To the Teacher. — Do not require children in this grade to give the meaning of the different prefixes and suffixes.

LESSON VIII.
Information Exercise.
COTTON.

Cotton-seed was planted as an experiment by some of the earliest settlers of the Southern States; but the plant was little known, except as a garden ornament, until after the Revolution.

About a hundred years ago the first Sea-Island cotton was raised on the coast of Georgia. The seeds were obtained from the Bahamas, having been introduced there from the West Indies.

COTTON FIELD.

The seed of the cotton is planted in March or April. The plants grow rapidly, and reach a height of from three to five feet. Later on, when the pale-yellow flowers drop off, a triangular pod is left. This ripens during the latter part of summer, and, bursting open, shows the white cotton, in which are hidden black or green seeds according to the variety. Cotton-seed yields an oil which is sometimes used in place of olive oil.

Topics for Study and Conversation.

When and where was cotton first raised in this country? Finest variety? — where from? — why so called?
Planting seeds, — blossom, — pod, or boll.
Cotton seeds, — cotton-gins, — Eli Whitney.
Uses of cotton, — cotton clothing, — cotton factories.

LESSON IX.
Composition.

Write what you have learned about cotton, following the order of the "Topics for Study" in Lesson VIII.

LESSON X.
Homonyms.

Supply the homonym for each of the following words:

scene	steak	rote ....
scent	weighed	heir ....
seize	weight	aisle ....
cell	waist	altar ....

1. Use in a sentence each word in the printed list, or tell its meaning.

2. Use in a sentence, or tell the meaning of, each word that you have supplied.

3. Review the lesson on homonyms, in Chapter Seven.

LESSON XI.
Dictation Exercise.

A humming-bird met a butterfly, and, being pleased with the beauty of his person and the glory of his wings, made an offer of perpetual friendship.

"I cannot think of it," was the reply, "as you once spurned me, and called me a drawling dolt."

"Impossible!" exclaimed the humming-bird. "I have always had the highest respect for such beautiful creatures as you."

"Perhaps you have now," said the other, "but when you insulted me I was a caterpillar. So, let me give you a piece of advice. Never insult the humble, as they may some day become your superiors."

LESSON XII.
Oral and written.

1. Tell the meaning of the following words selected from Lesson XI., or use each in a sentence: — *person, glory, perpetual, reply, spurned, drawling dolt, impossible, exclaimed, respect, insulted, advice, humble, superiors.*

2. Change direct quotations to indirect.

3. Re-write the entire dictation exercise, expressing the same thoughts without using any of the words whose meaning is asked for, and using only indirect quotations.

4. What *synonyms* have you used for any words in Lesson XI.?

LESSON XIII.
Verb-forms.

Write four derivative words from each of the following root-words: —*freeze, fall, see, write, grow.*

Example: freeze, freezes, freezing, froze, frozen.

1. After completing the five sets of words, notice how the second and third words in each set are made from the first.
2. Use in a sentence the fourth word in each set.
3. After what words is the fifth word generally used?
4. Use in a sentence the last word in each set.
5. Review Lesson XIV., in Chapter Seven.

NOTE. — See Lesson V., Chapter Six.

LESSON XIV

A Letter.

Robert Austin lives in Providence, R. I., where he is attending the Oxford Grammar School. His cousin, George Eliot, lives in a country town in New Jersey. Robert is getting tired of school-work, and is looking forward to vacation, when he hopes his cousin will visit him. So he writes to George, invites him to come, and suggests some of his plans for the vacation.

1. Make notes from which Robert's letter could be written.

To the Teacher. — From the notes made by the class, select such as seem most suggestive, and write them on the blackboard. Require all the pupils, at first, to write from the same notes.

2. Write Robert's letter in full.

LESSON XV.

Words often Misused.

Like for as.

As is correctly used in the following sentences:
Try to write *as* I do.
James is tall and straight, *as* his father was.

Few worse errors in English can be made than to use *like* instead of *as* in such sentences as the foregoing.

LANGUAGE EXERCISES. 111

Complete each of the following sentences with *like* or *as:*

My brother looks .... me.
I wish I could talk .... you do.

Make two sentences, in each of which *like* shall be used correctly.

Make two sentences, in each of which *as* shall be used correctly.

Funny for *odd* or *strange*.

The root of *funny* is *fun*. So, whatever is *funny* should make us laugh or feel pleased. Supply the proper word in each of the following sentences:

Uncle John told very .... stories to make us all laugh.
A camel is a .... looking animal.
The man had a very .... gait.

Most for *almost*.

Supply the proper words in the following sentences:

.... boys like apples.
We are .... there.
.... all of us prefer to speak correctly.
He said that he was .... well again.
My lesson is .... as hard as yours.

LESSON XVI.
Spelling Exercise.

The following exercises will show you how to study a spelling-lesson. You should prepare the lessons on your slate, or with paper and pencil.

gut ter	at tic	car riage	gim let
may or	pitch er	cof fee	vel vet
sa loon	bu reau	sir up	cam bric
gar ret	scis sors	vin e gar	cal i co
pi az za	cur tain	hatch et	en vel ope

1. Arrange the words alphabetically.
2. Classify them as to syllables.
3. Use each word in a thoughtful sentence.
4. Write a few sentences about "vinegar."

LESSON XVII.

Spelling Exercise.

an gel	stom ach	writ ten	birth day
sail or	fin ger	in di rect	doubt ful
schol ar	trou sers	re al ly	swin dle
mo ment	stock ing	mild ly	cin na mon
tor pe do	shoul der	cush ion	im ag ine

1. Which words are accented on the first syllable?
2. Which are accented on the last syllable?
3. Which words are derivatives, and from what words are they derived?
4. Write four or five lines about "torpedoes."

To the Teacher. — Pupils may do any or all of the work required in Lessons XVI. and XVII. in connection with any spelling-lesson that may be given. The object is to secure a correct knowledge of words by an intelligent use of them.

LESSON XVIII.

Synonyms.

In the second list of words below, a synonym may be found for each word in the first list:

1. Allow, imitate, feast, clumsy, detect, consume, border, construct, behavior, expensive, damage, cheat.

2. Awkward, costly, injury, deceive, devour, discover, conduct, banquet, build, edge, mimic, permit.

LANGUAGE EXERCISES.

1. Write each word with its synonym.
2. Use each word in the first list in a thoughtful sentence.
3. In which of your sentences may the synonyms be substituted without changing the meaning?

Example: *consume* and *devour* are synonyms.

A bear will *consume* a great deal of meat.
A bear will *devour* a great deal of meat.
A boy will sometimes *consume* much time in doing little work, but he will not *devour* the time.

LESSON XIX.

Words to use after *is* and *was*.

The following sentences are correct:

1. Was it *he* who spoke to *me?*
2. It was *I* who spoke to *him*.
3. Is it *she* who is talking to *us?*
4. It is *we* who are talking to *her*.
5. It is *they* who are to blame, and I blame *them*.

Complete the following sentences with one of the words in italics in the first five sentences:

1. Who is there? It is . . . .
2. Is it . . . . that you wish to see?
3. I know it was . . . . because I saw . . . .
4. Do you think it was . . . . ? No, it was . . . .
5. It is . . . . who were speaking to . . . .
6. Did you call . . . . ? No, it was . . . . that called you.
7. Who is there? It is only . . . . You need not be afraid of . . . .
8. That is my mother. I know it is . . . . I hear . . . . calling.

114 LANGUAGE EXERCISES.

9. Father, was that you? Yes, Charlie, it was .... Come to ....

10. Who sang "Home, Sweet Home"? It was .... and .... who sang it.

To the Teacher. — Review this topic frequently by means of oral questions.

LESSON XX.

A Letter.

Clara Fay attends a private school in Kingston, Ohio. She has been away from her home in Nashville, Tenn., nearly six months, and is looking forward, impatiently, to vacation, when she will once more see her father and mother. Her school is a very good one, and she is much attached to some of her school-mates.

1. Make the notes from which a letter might be written to her mother.
2. Write Clara's letter in full.
3. Draw and direct the envelope.

NOTE. — Her father is a physician living at 110 Regent St., Nashville.

To the Teacher. — See note, Lesson III., Chapter Eight.

LESSON XXI.

Combining two or more sentences into one.

1. Maine is the largest of the New England States.
   Maine is noted for its lumber.
2. Portland is the largest city in Maine.
   Portland was the birthplace of Longfellow.
   Longfellow was a famous American poet.
3. Washington served his country in the Revolution.
   Washington served his country as President.
   Washington retired to Mount Vernon.
   Mount Vernon is on the Potomac River.

4. John Adams was the second President of the United States.
John Adams was the father of John Quincy Adams.
John Quincy Adams was the sixth President of the United States.

5. Annie Johnson found a pocket-book.
The pocket-book was made of seal-skin.
It contained ten dollars.
Annie was on her way home from school.

6. Lake Champlain was once the scene of a famous battle.
Lake Champlain lies between New York and Vermont.

7. William Cullen Bryant was a poet.
He was editor of the New York *Evening Post* for fifty years.
He died at the age of eighty-four in New York.

8. General Harrison served in the civil war with great credit.
He also served in Congress as a Senator.
He was afterwards elected President.

LESSON XXII.

Study and commit to memory the following beautiful poem:

NOBILITY.

1. True worth is in *being*, not *seeming*,—
In doing, each day that goes by,
Some little good,— not in dreaming
Of great things to do by and by.
For, whatever men say in blindness,
And spite of the fancies of youth,
There's nothing so kingly as kindness,
And nothing so loyal as truth.

2. We get back our mete as we measure,
We cannot do wrong and feel right.
Nor can we give pain and feel pleasure,
For justice avenges each slight.

The air for the wing of the sparrow,
The bush for the robin and wren,
But alway the path that is narrow
And straight for the children of men.

3. We cannot make bargains for blisses,
   Nor catch them like fishes in nets;
And sometimes the thing our life misses
   Helps more than the thing which it gets.
For good lieth not in pursuing,
   Nor gaining of great nor of small;
But just in the doing, and doing
   As we would be done by, is all.

4. Through envy, through malice, through hating,
   Against the world, early and late,
No jot of our courage abating —
   Our part is to work and to wait.
And slight is the sting of his trouble
   Whose winnings are less than his worth;
For he who is honest is noble,
   Whatever his fortunes or birth.

ALICE CARY.

To the Teacher. — Study this poem very carefully with the children before they commit it to memory, and be sure that they appreciate its beautiful sentiments. Read with them the following or other poems selected from Alice Cary's writings: "Old Maxims," "Telling Fortunes," "The Wise Fairy," "Story of a Blackbird," "Waiting for Something to Turn Up," "Recipe for an Appetite," "In the Dark." See page 223.

Chapter Nine
Narratives.

You have already had considerable practice in writing compositions, and have learned something about the use of capital letters and punctuation marks. Some of your compositions have been called *stories*, some *letters*, and some *reproductions*.

Sometimes you will be called upon to describe what you have seen; and in order to do this well, you must notice very carefully every thing that will be likely to interest those who read your description.

If, for example, you wish to write an account of a game of base-ball that you have seen, you should first make full notes of the game and of such other matters connected with it as you would like to include in your account.

The notes given below may help you in the preparation of Lesson I. Study them carefully, and notice that they are so arranged as to suggest the number of paragraphs in the composition.

Notes.

A bright, sunshiny day. Saturday,— no school.
Our town boasts a famous "nine." The club that played with them to-day. How we went to the grounds. Rather hot and dusty. Incident.
Play begins. Our boys have bad luck. How the crowd screamed and whistled. Luck changes. Our boys ahead by one run. Umpire unfair. Game a tie.
Tenth inning decides it. Our boys beaten. The ride home. Better luck next time.

LESSON I.

Make notes for a composition on each of the following subjects:
1. A fishing excursion.
2. My visit to a menagerie.
3. My first attempt at skating.

LESSON II.

To the Teacher. — The notes which the pupils have made, as required in Lesson I., should be very carefully considered in the class. The most suggestive should be selected and written upon the blackboard, and afterwards arranged methodically by the pupils and teacher.

The value of descriptive or narrative compositions will depend very largely upon the accuracy and fullness of the notes.

From the three sets of notes written upon the blackboard select one set, and write a full account of the subject.

LESSON III.

Derivative Words.

Oral.

governor	misgovern	writer	rewriting
governing	ungovernable	rewrite	unwritten
government	misgovernment	written	rewritten

1. Name the root-word for each group of words.
2. In each word, name the prefix or suffix, or both.
3. Give the meaning of each word as nearly as you can.

Written.

1. Rewrite the words in each column, separating the root-word from the prefixes and suffixes.
2. Write sentences which shall show that you know the meaning of the root-words, and of all the derivatives.

To the Pupil. — In preparing for this lesson, read Lesson VII., Chapter Eight.

LESSON IV.
Dictation Exercise.

1. A rolling stone gathers no moss.
2. A bird in the hand is worth two in the bush.
3. Don't count your chickens before they are hatched.
4. Fine feathers do not make fine birds.
5. Birds of a feather flock together.
6. As you make your bed you must lie in it.
7. Handsome is that handsome does.
8. There's many a slip 'twixt the cup and the lip.
9. A tree is known by its fruit.
10. All that glitters is not gold.

Oral.

Explain in your own words the meaning of each of the foregoing proverbs and maxims.

To the Teacher.— In the dictation exercise, read each sentence distinctly and but once.

LESSON V.
Reproduction.

To the Teacher.— Read with the children Phœbe Cary's poem, "The Prairie on Fire." Be sure that the pictures of the poem are vividly impressed by means of a conversation exercise, and, after the preparation of topics, require a written reproduction of the scenes and the story.

The order below may be followed in the study of this poem:

1. Read with conversation and explanation.
2. Require the pupils to reproduce the substance of the poem in response to questions or hints by the teacher.
3. Require an oral reproduction without questions or hints from the teacher.
4. Require written reproduction from notes previously prepared in class.

Note.— These exercises will require two lessons at least.

LESSON VI.
Information Exercise.

WOOL.

The thick, soft hair on the skin of a sheep is called wool. This wool, if left to itself, would drop off in summer, for the sheep has then no need of it to keep him warm. But instead of allowing it to drop off, men cut it off just in time to save it. The wool sheared or cut from a sheep is called a *fleece*. The fleeces are cleaned and then sent to a factory, where the wool is spun into thread, and then woven into cloth.

Wool is obtained from other animals, such as the alpaca, cashmere goat, etc., but the sheep furnishes the greater part of that which is used in making clothing.

Topics for Study and Conversation.

Wool, what kind of product?
Sheep, different kinds, — some of the most valuable.

LANGUAGE EXERCISES. 121

Sheep-shearing, — explain the process.
Parts of our country where the most wool is produced.
Woolen manufactures. Worsteds.
Uses of wool and of woolen cloths.
What do you see in the picture, and what can you learn from it?

To the Teacher. — The conversation exercise above may be followed by a written exercise from the same notes, but the preparation for all written exercises should be made very carefully.

LESSON VII.

Homonyms.

After each of the following words write its homonym:

bred	grater	....	quartz	....
awl	flea	....	ore	....
dew	herd	....	reed	....
fir	....	lye	....	scull	....

1. Use in a sentence each word in the printed list.
2. Use in a sentence each word that you have supplied.
3. Use two or more of the words in one sentence.

LESSON VIII.

Pronunciation.

Pronounce the following words according to the marking:

mĭs′ chĭev oŭs	Fĕb′ rụ a rў̆	ēa′ sĭ lў̆
mĭs′ chĭev oŭs lў̆	găth′ er	sălm′ on (l silent)
fŏr′ ĕsts	sūġ ġĕst′	whĕth′ er
fōre′ hĕad (h silent)	ē lĕv′ en	wĭn′ dōw

1. In the first and second words, note carefully the accent.
2. In the third word, sound clearly the last two letters.

3. In the fifth word, sound the first *r*.
4. In the seventh, note the two sounds of *g*.
5. In the eleventh word, notice that the sound of *h* comes before the sound of *ĕ*.
6. Use each of these words so as to show that you know its meaning.

LESSON IX.
Conversation Exercise.
OUR OWN COUNTRY.

You have studied about "Cold Countries," and also about "Warm Countries." Now contrast our houses, our clothing, and our food, with the houses, clothing, and food of people living in cold countries, and also of people living in warm countries.

Contrast our modes of traveling and our manufactures with those of cold and of warm countries.

Give an account of any other advantages which you think we have over the people of those countries, and tell why you would rather live in our own country.

LESSON X.
Written Exercise.

Write about "Our own Country," and use as notes the hints found in the conversation exercise in Lesson IX.

LESSON XI.
Verb-forms.

1. From each of the following root-words form a derivative by adding *s* or *es*: — *bring, begin, blow, come, catch.*
2. Form a derivative from each by adding *ing*.
3. What name may you give to the parts added?

4. From each word form a derivative which may be used after *have, has,* or *had.*

5. What derivative from each word might be used in telling an event that took place last week?

6. Construct a table for your words like that in Lesson V., Chapter Six.

7. Use each of the words in your fourth and fifth columns in a sentence.

8. Review Lesson XIII., Chapter Eight.

To the Teacher.—Caution the pupils about the *spelling* when *ing* is added.

LESSON XII.

Letter-Writing (*Continued*).

To the Teacher.—Letter-writing can be made both interesting and profitable by combining it with the pupil's studies in geography. When a section of any country has been carefully studied, assume that the pupils are living in that section, and require them to write letters to friends, telling interesting facts concerning the country and its inhabitants, productions, etc.

Answers to such letters may also be written, in which pupils give facts concerning their own country, or part of the country, which would be likely to prove of interest to their correspondents.

In all cases make the preparation of such letters the subject of conversation with the pupils, and prepare full notes as suggested in previous lessons.

The following letter is given merely as a specimen of what may be done in this and the following grades.

Study the letter below, and make the notes from which it was written.

PAXTON, Ill., Oct. 14, 1888.

My dear Cousin,—

As I sit at my window writing, I am thinking that you, who live so many miles away among the hills of New England, may never have seen one of these vast western prairies.

Can you imagine a whole township of land, yes, many

townships, perhaps, as level as the floor in your father's barn, and entirely destitute of trees or even of shrubs? Well, our prairies in this neighborhood seem perfectly flat, and there is not a tree to be seen except now and then a few which have been planted by the settlers. Even stones are seldom found, and one may travel many a mile without seeing even a pebble in the black soil of our dusty roads.

I have been told that these prairies were once under water, — that they were the beds of great seas; but I am not wise enough really to know whether these sayings are true or not. I do know, however, that you would like to see these great plains, which must look so much like the vast ocean of which you speak. Some of the western prairies are called rolling prairies, because they look like the sea when it is in motion. I have seen such prairies myself many miles away, in another State.

Sometime I will tell you about the wheat, corn, rye, and oats that grow here; but I forget,—you must have learned about these things in your Geography.

Well, dear cousin, if I have told you nothing but what you knew before, at least I have kept my promise to write you a long letter. Now please write me all about your New-England hills, and remember that I have never seen them.

Your loving cousin, MAMIE.

LESSON XIII.

Preparation for Letter-Writing.

Prepare the notes for a letter in answer to the one written by Cousin Mamie, in Lesson XII.

Write your letter to Cousin Mamie in full.

To the Teacher. — Letters like the foregoing must follow lessons in geography, in which the pupils are required to give accurate information of the country which they are to describe.

LESSON XIV.
Synonyms.

1. From the following list of words select the synonyms, and place them in pairs: — *forsake, hasten, plentiful, desert, adieu, abundant, pleasant, collect, plenty, agreeable, abundance, hurry, beautify, affix, wealth, forgive, gather, adorn, skillful, pardon, annex, riches, farewell, clever.*

2. Use one of each pair of words in a sentence, and tell whether the sentence expresses exactly the same meaning when the other word is substituted.

3. Can you name a third synonym for any of the words?

LESSON XV.
Study of a Picture.

First *oral* and then *written.*

1. Describe the picture, telling what you see in it and what it suggests to you.

126 LANGUAGE EXERCISES.

2. Tell what you know about Indians, — their color, appearance, disposition, and manner of life. Describe the appearance of this country when the Indians possessed it.

3. Tell any story that you have heard or read about Indians.

NOTE. — In describing a picture, we use the words *foreground, background, center, right,* and *left.*

LESSON XVI.

Words often Misused.

Will for *shall.*

In asking questions, *will* should not be used before *I* or *we.* Complete the following sentences with the proper word:

1. Where .... we go when school is out?
2. .... I bring the book to you?
3. When the work is done, what .... I do?
4. .... we ever learn to use *shall* correctly?

Can for *may.*

May should be used either in asking or granting permission. We *can* do what we have strength or ability to do. Supply the proper word in the following sentences:

1. Mrs. Gray, ... I take your pencil? Certainly you ....
2. I should like to go home now; .... I?
3. I .... solve that problem; .... you?

Less for *fewer.*

Less should be used in speaking of *quantity;* as, less noise, less water.

Fewer should be used in speaking of *number;* as, fewer horses, fewer minutes.

LANGUAGE EXERCISES. 127

Complete the following sentences with the correct words:

1. There are .... boys than girls in our school, but the girls make .... noise than the boys.
2. I have .... credit marks than Mary, because I have spent .... time in study.
3. The .... water there is in the pond the .... fish there will be.

Construct three questions, showing the correct use of *shall*.
Construct three questions, showing the correct use of *may*.
Construct three statements, each of which shall contain *less* and *fewer* properly used.

LESSON XVII.
Paraphrase.

The thoughts which a writer has expressed in prose or poetry may be expressed by changing the form of what he has written. This change in expression is called *paraphrase*. The most common paraphrase consists in changing poetry into prose. This may be done by using very nearly the same words, or by expressing the thoughts in almost entirely different language. You have already done much of this kind of work in connection with reproductions of stories, where you have been required to tell, *in your own words*, the substance of what you have read. The stanza below, with the following statements of the meaning in prose, will illustrate what is meant by paraphrasing: —

> Under a spreading chestnut-tree
> The village smithy stands;
> The smith — a mighty man is he,
> With large and sinewy hands;
> And the muscles of his brawny arms
> Are strong as iron bands.
>
> HENRY W. LONGFELLOW.

LANGUAGE EXERCISES.

1. The village smithy stands under a spreading chestnut-tree. The smith is a mighty man, and he has large and sinewy hands. His brawny arms have muscles as strong as iron bands.

2. The blacksmith shop of the village stands under a large chestnut-tree whose branches almost cover it. The blacksmith is a man of great strength. The work which he does has made his hands very large, and the muscles of his arm are almost as strong as iron.

You will see that the first paraphrase was made with very little change in Mr. Longfellow's words, while in the last the words were changed very freely.

1. Make a paraphrase of the following stanzas, using nearly the same words.

2. Explain fully in your own words the meaning of each stanza.

1. Build me straight, O worthy master,—
   Stanch and strong, a goodly vessel
   That shall laugh at all disaster,
   And with wave and whirlwind wrestle.
              From "Building of the Ship," by LONGFELLOW.

2. New are the leaves on the oaken spray,
   New the blades of the silky grass;
   Flowers, that were buds but yesterday,
   Peep from the ground where'er I pass.
              From "The New and the Old," by BRYANT.

3. The glance that doth thy neighbor doubt,
   Turn thou, O man, within,
   And see if it will not bring out
   Some unsuspected sin.
              ALICE CARY.

LESSON XVIII.

Commit to memory the following poem, by Oliver Wendell Holmes, and try to interpret its meaning, as a preparation for the fuller study outlined in the next lesson:

THE OLD MAN DREAMS.

1. Oh for one hour of youthful joy!
    Give back my twentieth spring!
    I'd rather laugh a bright-haired boy,
    Than reign a gray-beard king.

2. Off with the spoils of wrinkled age!
    Away with learning's crown!
    Tear out life's wisdom-written page,
    And dash its trophies down.

3. One moment let my life-blood stream
    From boyhood's fount of flame!
    Give me one giddy, reeling dream
    Of life all love and fame.
    . . . . . .

4. My listening angel heard the prayer,
    And, calmly smiling, said,
    "If I but touch thy silvered hair,
    Thy hasty wish hath sped."

5. "But is there nothing in thy track,
    To bid thee fondly stay,
    While the swift seasons hurry back,
    To find the wished-for day?"

6. "Ah, truest soul of womankind!
    Without thee what were life!

One bliss I cannot leave behind :
I'll take — my — precious — wife."

7. The angel took a sapphire pen
And wrote in rainbow dew,
*The man would be a boy again,
And be a husband too!*

8. "And is there nothing yet unsaid
Before the change appears?
Remember, all their gifts have fled
With those dissolving years."

9. "Why, yes;" for memory would recall
My fond paternal joys;
"I could not bear to leave them all —
I'll take — my — girl — and — boys."

10. The smiling angel dropped his pen, —
"Why, this will never do;
The man would be a boy again,
And be a father too."

. . . . . .

11. And so I laughed, — my laughter woke
The household with its noise, —
And wrote my dream, when morning broke,
To please the gray-haired boys.

OLIVER WENDELL HOLMES.

LESSON XIX.

Study of the Poem.

1. Who speaks in the first three stanzas?
2. What does the speaker want?
3. What is meant by the last two verses of the first stanza?

LANGUAGE EXERCISES. 131

4. What is meant by "the spoils of wrinkled age"? by "learning's crown"?
5. What "prayer" is referred to in the fourth stanza?
6. Who speaks in the last half of the fourth stanza?
7. Tell in your own language what he says.
8. What is the meaning of the question asked in the fifth?
9. Who speaks in the sixth stanza? Name all the words in the sixth that refer to *wife*.
10. Give the meaning of the seventh.
11. Who speaks in the eighth stanza? Why is the question asked? Why does he say "remember"?
12. Who speaks in the ninth? Give what is said, in your own words.
13. Explain the tenth stanza.
14. Who are the "gray-haired boys"?

LESSON XX.

Composition.

Write the story of "The Old Man Dreams," and tell who the old man was.

To the Teacher.—Read with the children, and talk about, the following of Holmes's poems: "To an Insect," "Lexington," "The Deacon's Masterpiece," "Grandmother's Story of Bunker-Hill Battle." See page 223.

132   *LANGUAGE EXERCISES.*

CHAPTER TEN.

LESSON I.

Topics for Study and Conversation.

1. Birthplace and family of Henry W. Longfellow.
2. Boyhood. "My Lost Youth."
3. College life, and famous classmates.
4. Professor in college.
5. His home at Cambridge, and his family.

LANGUAGE EXERCISES. 133

6. His travels in Europe.
7. His writings. First poem.
8. The " Children's Arm-Chair."
9. Longfellow's love for children. "Children," "Children's Hour," "Weariness."
10. The celebration of his seventy-fifth birthday. Whittier's poem.
11. Longfellow's death and burial.

LESSON II.

Biographical Sketch.

Write what you have learned in Lesson I. about Mr. Longfellow. Follow the order of the notes in that lesson, and divide your composition into paragraphs.

LESSON III.

Words often Mispronounced.

wharf	truths	prē tĕnse'	dĕṣ ṣērt'
wōn't	rĭnse	mŭs täche'	grēaṣ' ĭng
yŏn' der	rĭsk	ō' á sĭs	ĭn quīr' ў

After studying the words carefully, write them upon slates or paper without marking them. Then test your ability to answer the following questions on pronunciation, and mark your words without the aid of the book.

1. What sound has *o* in the second word?
2. Why is *th* not marked in the fourth word?
3. Name the vowel sound in the fifth and sixth.
4. Which is the accented syllable in the seventh, eighth, ninth, tenth, twelfth?
5. In the eighth what sound has *ch*?
6. What sound has *s* in the ninth?

7. What is the plural of the ninth word?
8. What sound has each *s* in the tenth?
9. What sound has *s* in the eleventh?
10. Name the sound of *i* in each syllable of the twelfth.
11. Which words are derivatives? What are their root-words?
12. Pronounce the words from the book.
13. Use each word in a thoughtful sentence, and, in giving the sentence, speak the required word very distinctly.

To the Teacher. — Always review one or more similar lessons on pronunciation, if there is time.

LESSON IV.

Dictation Exercise.

Study the meaning of the following verses, and the manner of writing them. They were selected from Longfellow's poems. After writing the sentences, explain their full meaning in you own words.

1. Our to-days and yesterdays
   Are the blocks with which we build.

2. Go to the woods and hills: no tears
   Dim the sweet look that Nature wears.

3. Ah! what would the world be to us
   If the children were no more.

4. Into each life some rain must fall,
   Some days must be dark and dreary.

5. A wind came out of the sea
   And said, "O mists, make room for me!"

6. Something attempted, something done,
   Has earned a night's repose.

LANGUAGE EXERCISES. 135

7. Blow winds! and waft through all the rooms
The snow-flakes of the cherry-blooms.

8. Dust thou art, to dust returnest,
Was not spoken of the soul.

To the Teacher. — If desirable, this lesson may be divided into two or even three dictation exercises.

LESSON V.
Homonyms.

After each of the following words write its homonym:

seam	beach	current ....
shone	cellar	flue ....
soul	corps	whoop ....
bass	creek	mail ....

1. Use in a sentence each word in the foregoing list.
2. Use in a sentence each word which you have supplied.
3. Define as many of the words in each list as you can. Make the definitions exact.
4. Many people never learn to use the homonyms *there*, *their*, and *to, too, two*, correctly. Write sentences to prove that you can use these five words correctly.

LESSON VI.
A Letter.

Suppose that you are now living in some warm country about which you have studied in your Geography. Prepare notes, and then write a letter to a friend living where you do now.

To the Teacher. — See suggestions in Lesson XII., Chapter Nine.

LANGUAGE EXERCISES.

LESSON VII.

Synonyms.

Each of the first three words in the following list has one synonym in the columns below. Each of the second three words has two synonyms: — *exact, loitered, discuss, fold, hale, dismal.*

dreary	gloomy	envelop
lingered	argue	correct
healthy	robust	wrap

1. Arrange the synonyms in twos or threes as the case may be.
2. Study the synonyms; first, think how they are alike in meaning; and, second, think how they differ.
3. In the following sentences, decide whether the meaning would be changed if the synonyms were used for the words in italics:

1. Our teacher is very *exact* in his language.
2. *Fold* your letter and place it in the envelope.
3. A *hale* old man of seventy is pleasant to meet.
4. The little boy *lingered* near the door, as he wished to apologize for his conduct.
5. People *discuss* questions freely just before election.
6. "The day is cold and dark and *dreary.*"

LESSON VIII.

Oral Paraphrase or Conversation.

NOTE. — The following stanzas were selected from Longfellow's poems:

1. I heard the bells on Christmas-day
    Their old familiar carols play,

And wild and sweet the woods repeat
   Of peace on earth, good-will to men.
                        From "Christmas Bells."

2. Somewhat back from the village street
Stands the old-fashioned country-seat.
Across its antique portico
Tall poplar-trees their shadows throw,
And, from its station in the hall,
An ancient time-piece says to all,
   " Forever — never
      Never —forever."
               From "The Old Clock on the Stairs."

3. This is the Arsenal. From floor to ceiling
   Like a huge organ rise the burnished arms;
But from their silent pipes no anthem, pealing,
   Startles the villagers with strange alarms.
                  From "The Arsenal at Springfield."

4. Out of the bosom of the Air,
   Out of the cloud-folds of her garments shaken,
Over the woodland brown and bare,
   Over the harvest fields forsaken,
      Silent, and soft, and slow,
      Descends the snow.
                        From "Snow-Flakes."

5. By the fireside there are peace and comfort,
Wives and children with fair, thoughtful faces,
         Waiting, watching
For a well-known footstep in the passage.
               From "The Golden Mile-Stone."

6. Often I think of the beautiful town
   That is seated by the sea;

Often in thought go up and down
The pleasant streets of that dear old town,
And my youth comes back to me.
From "My Lost Youth."

To the Teacher.—In the preparation of this lesson, ask the children to commit to memory the stanza that seems to them most beautiful or thoughtful, each to decide for himself. The class exercise should of course include the recitation of the extracts selected. Encourage the children to read the poems containing the stanzas, and ask them for any additional thoughts from the poems read. The primary object of such lessons is to lead children to appreciate and love the beautiful, both in thought and in expression. If expedient the lesson may be divided into two or three exercises.

LESSON IX.

Information Exercise.

Read the following account, and gather from every possible source information about cocoons. The more carefully you make the preparation, the better will be your composition which is to follow.

THE COCOON.

Many insects begin life as little worms. Every few days these little worms change their skins. Some of them change them four times, and then are ready to spin their cocoons. The little worm—which is now full grown—attaches itself to something by its hind feet, and then throws out from its mouth a continuous thread, which it manages to wind round and round itself until it is completely covered. This thread, which forms the cocoon of the silk-worm, is several miles long.

After lying in the cocoon a certain length of time, the change is completed and a moth bursts forth. If a female, it soon deposits its eggs, and dies after a short life of three or four days. The male lives about the same length of time.

Of course, you have all seen the cocoons of moths and butterflies, which are often fastened under window-sills or fence-rails or upon the limbs of trees; and many of you have put them into boxes and have seen the beautiful moths or butterflies come out of them.

To the Teacher.— Encourage the children to collect cocoons, and keep them in the school-room while the insect is undergoing its transformation; or, better still, confine the worms which make cocoons, in large bottles or inverted tumblers, and see the cocoons made. Be sure that the pupils get all the information they can by their own observation.

One object in giving such lessons is to induce the children to become careful observers.

LESSON X.

Composition.

Prepare notes, and then write what you have learned about cocoons.

LESSON XI.

Review.

1. Name five nouns that form the plural by adding *es*.
2. Name two nouns ending in *o* that form the plural by adding *s*.
3. Name three dissyllables ending in *y* that form the plural by adding *s*. Name three nouns ending in *y* whose plurals end in *ies*.
4. Name three nouns ending in *f* or *fe* that form their plurals by adding *s*. Name three nouns ending in *f* or *fe* whose plurals end in *ves*.
5. Mention and illustrate two uses of the period.
6. What letters are always vowels?

7. Illustrate five different sounds of *a* in five different words. Mark *a* in each word. Name the five sounds.

8. Illustrate in the same way, mark, and name two sounds of *e*, two sounds of *i*, four sounds of *o*, four sounds of *u*, and two sounds of *oo*.

9. *C* may represent the sounds of three different letters. Name the letters. Illustrate. Has *c* any sound of its own?

10. Represent the sound of long *oo* in three different ways in different words.

LESSON XII.
Verb-forms.

Each of the following words will suggest four other words, making five forms in all. Arrange the forms of the several words in a table similar to those in previous lessons, and number the columns 1, 2, 3, 4, 5.

In answering the following questions, you may speak of the forms as first, second, third, etc., numbering them from the columns in which they stand.

ring   *shake*   *drink*   *speak*   *steal*

1. Which forms are made by means of the suffix *ing?*
2. Which forms end in *s?*
3. Before which of the forms can the word *to* be used?
4. Before which forms can *have, has, had,* be used?
5. Use in sentences the words in the fourth column.
6. Use in sentences the words in the fifth column.

Review.

Use the following words in sentences: — *begun, blew, came, blown, frozen, fell, seen, wrote, grew, saw, fallen, began, grown, written, went, drawn, forgot, given, flew, done, broke, eaten, did, flown, gave, broken, gone, forgotten, ate, come.*

LESSON XIII.

Information Exercise.

THE SILK-WORM.

The silk-worm is hatched from the egg of a kind of moth. The egg is about the size of a mustard-seed. The worm comes out in a few days if the weather is warm and dry. When it is between three and four weeks old it begins to spin its cocoon, for it is now time for it to go to sleep, and a nice warm hiding-place must be made.

Usually it takes only a few hours for the silk-worm to spin its cocoon, but sometimes two or three days are required. In about two weeks in warm climates, or nearly two months in cold, the cocoon opens at one end, and out comes — not the worm, but a whitish colored moth.

The cocoon of the silk-worm is very valuable, for it is made of a fine silk thread, which can be unwound and spun into silk, of which articles of clothing are made.

Topics for Study.

Eggs, — where laid, size, etc. The worm, — spinning the cocoons. The moth. When the cocoons are collected and how treated. Silk manufacture.

To the Teacher. — The "Topics for Study" must be considered in a conversation exercise, because most pupils will be unable to find books from which to gather the necessary information.

LESSON XIV.
Composition.

Make notes of what you have learned about the silk-worm, and afterwards write as full an account of the subject as you can.

LESSON XV.
Words often Misused.
Cute.

Cute is an abbreviation for *acute*. It means clever or sharp. So when people speak of a *cute* baby, they should mean a *sharp* baby.

Cute is not a good word to use in any sense, although it is very common.

In and *into.*

Explain the difference in the meanings of the following sentences:

The boy ran in the house.
The boy ran into the house.

LANGUAGE EXERCISES. 143

The man carried the potatoes into the cellar.
The man carried the potatoes in the cellar.

In the following sentences supply *in* or *into:*

1. I jumped from the boat .... the water.
2. Will you come .... the school-house? I am .... it now.
3. The woman ran from the house .... the street.

Cupola, Balustrade, Baluster.

Notice that *cupola* ends in *a*, and that *o* is in the second syllable of the word.

Almost every flight of stairs has a *balustrade*. Boys sometimes slide down the railing of a balustrade.

The rounds upon which the railing of a balustrade rests are *balusters*.

To the Teacher. — Engage the children in conversation about the words presented in this lesson until their use is thoroughly understood. Review similar lessons in preceding chapters.

LESSON XVI.

Composition.

To the Teacher. — Read carefully with the children Longfellow's poem, "The Village Blacksmith." See that the pictures in the poem, and the lesson in the last stanza are brought vividly to the minds of the pupils, and given by them in oral recitation. Then tell them of the incident which led to the writing of "My Arm-Chair," and read this poem also in class.

A composition may follow, which shall tell what they have learned from and about, the two poems. It would be a pleasant feature of the exercise if each composition should contain an extract from one of the poems.

LESSON XVII.

Derivatives.

Root-words are often called *primitive* words or *primitives*. The root of the word *primitive* is *prime*, which means

144 LANGUAGE EXERCISES.

first. Hence the *primitive* word is the *first* word, and from it the derivative is formed.

Study carefully the following lists of derivative words:

faithful	civilized	careless	monosyllable
faithfully	civilly	careful	dissyllable
faithless	uncivil	carelessly	trisyllable
unfaithful	uncivilly	carefully	syllabicate

1. Name the root or primitive word in each set of words.
2. Name the prefixes and suffixes in each set.
3. Define the words or use them in sentences.
4. Copy the several sets of words, separating the roots from the prefixes and suffixes.

LESSON XVIII.

A Letter.

July 7, 1888, Delia Morris writes to her friend Helen Winship, giving an account of the annual exhibition of her school in Cleveland, Ohio.

She begins her letter by saying that she would have written before, had not the pleasures as well as the cares of the recent Fourth prevented.

Her school closed on the last Friday in June with a grand exhibition, in which she took an active part. She describes the decorations of the hall, the company, noted persons present, and finally the exercises of the pupils and the closing ceremonies.

Think out each portion of the account which Delia Morris's letter may have contained, and then write the letter in full.

Have a distinct picture in your own mind of the entire scene, and then try to describe it in such words as will

LANGUAGE EXERCISES. 145

convey the picture to the mind of the reader. If possible, introduce some humorous incident to add *spice* to your letter.

To the Teacher.—Prepare the pupils for this work by a carefully conducted conversation exercise.

LESSON XIX.
Conversation Exercise.

1. Describe the foregoing picture fully, and tell what you think of the family.

2. The picture was suggested by the most famous book that has ever been written for boys. If you have read the book, tell what you know about the story. If not, read it before this school year is over.

LESSON XX.

Dictation Exercise.

MAXIMS AND PROVERBS.

To the Teacher. — Read each sentence distinctly and but once.

1. Charity begins at home.
2. A drowning man will catch at a straw.
3. Beggars must not be choosers.
4. Cut your coat according to your cloth.
5. Every rose has its thorn.
6. Fair exchange is no robbery.
7. A stitch in time saves nine.
8. Great oaks from little acorns grow.
9. Honesty is the best policy.
10. Try to hit the nail on the head.
11. He does much who does well what he has to do.
12. Never cross a bridge till you come to it.
13. Paddle your own canoe.
14. The early bird catches the worm.
15. Where there's a will, there's a way.

After writing and, if necessary, correcting the foregoing sentences, give your idea orally of the meaning of each. The lesson should be well studied.

LESSON XXI.

Review.

1. State two uses of the apostrophe and illustrate.
2. What is a direct quotation? How is it written?
3. In what sort of quotation are no quotation marks used?
4. Tell whether there is a quotation in the following sentence, and if so what kind of quotation: George wrote his mother that he had recently visited Niagara Falls, and

LANGUAGE EXERCISES. 147

that his pleasure would have been complete had she been with him.

5. Prove that there is a quotation in 4, by changing the sentence. Explain the effect of the change.

6. Where do you use the comma in writing the heading of a letter? the salutation? the close?

7. Write two sentences which will illustrate other uses of the comma.

8. What are synonyms? What are homonyms?

9. What is meant by paraphrase?

10. What is the root of the word *classify*? What does the word mean? In what cases have you been required to classify words?

LESSON XXII.

Study and commit to memory the following poem:

CHILDREN.

1. Come to me, O ye children!
  For I hear you at your play,
  And the questions that perplexed me
  Have vanished quite away.

2. Ye open the eastern windows,
  That look towards the sun,
  Where thoughts are singing swallows
  And the brooks of morning run.

3. In your hearts are the birds and the sunshine,
  In your thoughts the brooklets flow,
  But in mine is the wind of Autumn,
  And the first fall of the snow.

4. Ah! what would the world be to us
  If the children were no more?

We should dread the desert behind us
Worse than the dark before.

5. What the leaves are to the forest,
With light and air for food,
Ere their sweet and tender juices
Have been hardened into wood, —

6. That to the world are children;
Through them it feels the glow
Of a brighter and sunnier climate
Than reaches the trunks below.

7. Come to me, O ye children!
And whisper in my ear
What the birds and the winds are singing
In your sunny atmosphere.

8. For what are all our contrivings,
And the wisdom of our books,
When compared with your caresses,
And the gladness of your looks.

9. Ye are better than all the ballads
That ever were sung or said;
For ye are living poems,
And all the rest are dead.

Henry W. Longfellow.

To the Teacher. — Of course a conversation exercise should accompany the learning of this beautiful poem. Re-read the poems suggested at the close of Chapter Six, and read "The Bell of Atri," and selections from "Hiawatha," "Evangeline," and the "Building of the Ship." Every boy and girl in America should study and commit to memory the concluding part of the last named poem.

Many other of Longfellow's short poems might be named, but the teacher's good taste will be sure to find them out.

PART III.

TO TEACHERS

ATTENTION has already been called to the memorizing of choice selections of poetry, and in succeeding chapters still greater stress will be laid upon the value of this feature of language-work. It is believed that too little time has been given, in the schools, to a careful study of the works of the best American authors. Much of our literature is within the comprehension of the pupils in our lower grades. Many of the thoughts find appropriate expression in language that is worthy of a permanent place in the memories of our children.

It would be difficult to over-estimate the influence for good of "memory gems" when permanently lodged in the mind and understanding of a child. Nor should we under-estimate their value for language-training. Gems of poetry or prose,—they are none the less *gems* because of the beauty of their setting,—when thoroughly memorized, keep constantly before our minds the highest ideals of expression, and such ideals constantly stimulate us to greater effort in the same direction.

Teachers are urged to study with the pupils the selections given in the book, and such others as may seem to them worthy of time and effort. Many pupils will hardly find all that is good in a poem without some assistance from a teacher; and frequently this assistance can best be given by suggesting collateral reading in the way of "side-lights." This supplementary reading, to which attention is called in many of the chapters, will contribute greatly to the language-training of the pupils.

LANGUAGE EXERCISES. 151

CHAPTER ELEVEN.
LESSON I.
Topics for Study and Conversation.
1. Whittier's birthplace and home circle. ("Snow-Bound.")
2. The Friends, or "Quakers."

LANGUAGE EXERCISES.

3. School life. Very limited advantages. How he earned money to pay his tuition. "In School Days." "My Playmate."
4. Effect of Robert Burns's poems.
5. Writing for newspapers. (Garrison.)
6. An editor.
7. Most famous poems.
8. His present home (1889), and his age.

To the Teacher.—The poems of Mr. Whittier are so simple in construction and so easily understood, that they are especially interesting to children. It will be very easy to select, for use in school, a large number of his poems from the lists given on page 223.

LESSON II.
Biographical Sketch of John G. Whittier.

Write what you have learned about Mr. Whittier, following the order of the topics in Lesson I.

LESSON III.
Dictation Exercise.

The following verses were selected from Whittier's poems:

1. Cheerily then my little man,
   Live and laugh as boyhood can.

2. Still let us for His golden corn
   Send up our thanks to God.

3. Who looking back from his manhood's prime
   Sees not the specter of his misspent time?

4. 'Tis the noon of the spring-time, yet never a bird
   In the wind-shaken elm or maple is heard.

5. Of all sad words of tongue or pen,
   The saddest are these, "It might have been."

6. What moistens the lips, what brightens the eye,
   What calls back the past like the rich pumpkin-pie?

7. Long live the good school! giving out year by year
   Recruits to true manhood and womanhood dear.

8. Ah! that thou couldst know thy joy
   Ere it passes, barefoot boy.

To the Teacher. — In preparation of the lesson, direct the children's attention to the thought as well as to the form of the couplets. The material for a conversation lesson, which should follow, is excellent. Many teachers prefer to have short dictation exercises. This lesson, or any other like it, may be divided into two or more shorter ones.

LESSON IV.
For Reproduction.
VALUATION.

1. The old Squire said, as he stood by his gate,
   And his neighbor, the Deacon, went by,
   "In spite of my bank stock and real estate,
   You are better off, Deacon, than I.

2. "We're both growing old and the end's drawing near,
   You have less of this world to resign,
   But, in heaven's appraisal, your assets, I fear,
   Will reckon up greater than mine.

3. "They say I am rich, but I'm feeling so poor,
   I wish I could swap with you even:
   The pounds I have lived for and laid up in store,
   For the shillings and pence you have given."

4. "Well, Squire," said the Deacon, with shrewd common-sense,
   While his eye had a twinkle of fun,
   "Let your pounds take the way of my shillings and pence,
   And the thing can be easily done."

JOHN G. WHITTIER.

Study carefully the foregoing poem and then write the incident in two paragraphs, using no direct quotations. Add a third paragraph, telling whether you think the Squire was sincere, and the reason for your opinion.

To the Teacher. — Let the recitation consist of the reading of several, or all, of the reproductions, and a conversation upon the third paragraph of the pupils' compositions.

LESSON V.
Exercise in Pronunciation.

In the lessons for pronunciation thus far in this book, the words have all been carefully marked. For the correct pronunciation of words in similar lessons in the remainder of the book, you must depend on the Dictionary.

fertile	extra	plague
gradually	gestures	launch
government	address	mountainous
illustrated	arithmetic	quinine

In preparation of the lesson, copy the words, and with the aid of your Dictionary divide them into syllables and mark the accented syllable in each. Then note carefully the marks of the letters, especially in the accented syllable, and you may be certain of the pronunciation of the word.

1. What sound has *i* in the first word?
2. What is the second syllable of the second word?
3. What is the root-word of the third? What is the last syllable?
4. Which syllable is accented in the fourth?
5. In the sixth is *g* hard or soft?
6. In the seventh, which syllable is *always* accented?
7. Give the sound of *a* in each monosyllable.

LANGUAGE EXERCISES. 155

8. Give the sounds of *i* in each syllable of the twelfth.
9. Name the derivatives and their primitive words.
10. Pronounce the words very distinctly.
11. Define each word, or use it in a thoughtful sentence.
12. Pronounce the words in Lesson III., Chapter Ten.

To the Teacher. — Frequent class exercises should be had in the quick finding of words in the Dictionary, and in the correct determination of pronunciation and appropriate definition. The Dictionary should be the constant hand-book of the pupil.

LESSON VI.
Preparation for Letter-Writing.

1. Imagine that you are living in Greenland, and have friends living where you do now.
2. Prepare notes from which you may write a letter to one of your friends. Arrange the notes so as to suggest the number of paragraphs.
3. Your letter should include an account of tne country, the climate, people, houses, food, modes of traveling, etc.

To the Pupil. — In the preparation of this letter you can get much assistance from books containing accounts of adventures in the Arctic regions. Such books may be found in any good library in your neighborhood.

LESSON VII.
Letter.

Write the letter in full from your notes prepared under Lesson VI. Arrange your paragraphs as suggested by your notes.

Review.

After you have written the letter above in full, you may write answers to the following questions:

1. What is the *heading* of your letter?
2. What information is given in the *heading*?

3. What is the *salutation* of your letter?
4. What words in the *salutation* begin with capitals, and why?
5. What is the *conclusion* of your letter?
6. What marks of punctuation have you used in the *conclusion ?*
7. Draw and direct the envelope.

LESSON VIII.

Abbreviations.

Anon., *Anonymous.*
inst., *this month.*
Jr., *Junior.*
M. D., *Doctor of Medicine.*
prox., *next month.*

Sr., *Senior.*
U. S. A., *United States Army.*
U. S. N., *United States Navy.*
ult., *last month.*
Viâ, *by the way of.*

Anonymous means "without name." It is written after any composition whose author is unknown.

The use of the fourth, seventh, and eighth abbreviations in the foregoing list is shown with the following names: S. E. Edwards, M. D.; Gen. W. T. Sherman, U. S. A.; Capt. Ericsson, U. S. N.

James Madison, Jr., is the son of James Madison, Sr.

The use of the three abbreviations *inst., prox.,* and *ult.* is shown in the following sentences: Lieut. Barry, U. S. N., is expected in New York on the 17th *inst.* He left Malta on the 15th *ult.*, and will leave for California on the 20th *prox.*

Viâ is not really an abbreviation, but a full Latin word.

1. Copy the abbreviations in the list, and write from memory the words for which they stand.
2. Use the abbreviations so as to show that you know their meaning.

LESSON IX.

Information Exercise.

To the Teacher. — Ask pupils to make a collection of shells along the shore of some lake or river. Some of the shells will be empty, or *dead shells*. These should be studied first. Each pupil in the class should be supplied with a shell, and taught to draw its form correctly in preparation for the following lesson.

Study the following description of a shell, and compare it with the best specimen you can find.

FRESH-WATER SNAIL-SHELLS.

Did you ever start at the top of a tall tower and walk around and around a winding, or spiral, staircase as you came down? The snail-shell is like that staircase. Beginning at the pointed top, or apex of the shell and following the spiral down, each complete twist around the shell is called a *whorl*. The line separating the whorls is the *suture*. All the whorls form a *spire*. Do you see why such shells are called spiral shells?

Following down from the apex you soon reach the doorway, where the snail puts out its head for food. This doorway is called the *aperture*. It is just here that the shell becomes larger as it grows.

To the Pupil. — After having studied the foregoing account of a fresh-water snail-shell, write in the proper places, upon the drawing which you have made, the words *apex*, *whorl*, *suture*, *spire*, and *aperture*.

Oral Exercise.

1. Have you ever seen a winding or spiral staircase?
2. Why do some shells remind you of such a staircase?
3. What is the *apex* of a shell?
4. What is the *whorl?* the *suture?* the *spire?*
5. Describe the doorway. Why is it called an *aperture?*

LESSON X.

Synonyms.

The following list contains twenty-four words. It is possible to arrange them in eight sets of three words each, so that the words in each set shall be synonyms. They are very common words, and you will probably be able to arrange them without assistance.

cunning	dwelling	idle	sly
knave	artful	lessen	residence
absurd	inform	speechless	decrease
mute	lazy	tell	silly
abode	notify	indolent	dumb
rogue	diminish	rascal	ridiculous

1. Use one of each set of words in a sentence.

2. Try the same sentence with each of the other words in the set, and tell whether the meaning is at all changed.

LESSON XI.

Verb-forms.

Make a table of the different forms of the following words:

take
tear
throw
choose
wear

To the Teacher. — When the forms are properly arranged, call attention to the formation of the words in the second and third columns, especially to the dropping of final *e* when *ing* is added. Then give close and varied practice in the use of the words in the fourth and fifth columns.

LESSON XII.

Study of a Picture.

Oral.

Topics for Study and Conversation.

1. Describe the foregoing picture, and tell of what great event in history it reminds you?

2. Tell what you know about this event, and of the persons and countries connected with it.

To the Teacher—A written exercise may follow the study of the picture.

LESSON XIII.

Oral Paraphrase.

STANZAS FROM WHITTIER'S POEMS.

1. A tender child of summers three,
    Seeking her little bed at night,
    Paused on the dark stair timidly.
    "Oh, mother! take my hand," said she,
    "And then the dark will all be light."
        From "The Light That is Felt."

2. What matter how the storm behaved?
What matter how the north wind raved?
Blow high, blow low, not all its snow
Could quench our hearth-fire's ruddy glow.
From "Snow-Bound."

3. Oh! for boyhood's time of June,
Crowding years in one brief noon,
When all things I heard or saw,
Me, their master, waited for.
From "The Barefoot Boy."

4. O land of lands! to thee we give
Our prayers, our hopes, our service free;
For thee thy sons shall nobly live,
And at thy need shall die for thee.
From "Our Country."

To the Teacher.— The conversation lesson on these stanzas should be full and free until the children thoroughly understand what is said or implied. Then each pupil may write a paraphrase of one stanza.

LESSON XIV.

Information Exercise.

FRESH-WATER SNAIL-SHELLS (Continued).

Examine your shell once more. Can you see some delicate lines running across the outside of the shell from one suture to the next? These lines are called lines of growth. As the snail grows, it finds that the shell is too small for its body; so it adds more and more to the rim of the shell, just as rows of bricks are added to a wall to make it higher.

The snail's shell is a part of the animal. The hard and the soft parts of the snail are so connected by muscles that the snail cannot leave its house. This grows with the other parts of the snail. Of what use is the shell?

LANGUAGE EXERCISES. 161

Drawing Exercise.

1. Make a sketch of a shell, and write the name of each part in its proper place.
2. Copy the following list of words:

apex	suture	lines of growth
whorl	spiral	shell
spire	aperture	muscle

3. Use each word in such way as to show your knowledge of its meaning.
4. Write any interesting facts that you have learned about shells.

To the Teacher. — Require the pupils to draw from a shell, if possible.

LESSON XV.
Homonyms.

Each of the following words has two homonyms. Copy the words and write the homonyms after each.

two	....	....	scent	....	....
pair	....	....	seize	....	....
rode	....	....	vein	....	....
reign	....	....	sew	....	....

To the Teacher. — After the sets of words are completed, ask for definitions of the words; or in case the definitions are not easy to give, ask for use in sentences. Then dictate sentences for the children to write, using one or more of the foregoing words or their homonyms. Or dictate sentences, and ask to have certain words written, or spelled orally.

LESSON XVI.
Dictation Exercise.
PROVERBS AND MAXIMS.

1. Don't cry for spilled milk.
2. If wishes were horses, beggars might ride.

3. It is a long road that has no turning.
4. Judge not that ye be not judged.
5. Jack at all trades and good at none.
6. Make hay while the sun shines.
7. Do not make a mountain out of a mole-hill.
8. People who live in glass houses should not throw stones.
9. Necessity is the mother of invention.
10. Riches have wings.
11. Strike while the iron is hot.
12. There is no royal road to learning.

In studying the foregoing lesson, think what each sentence means. After writing the sentence, you may be asked to tell the full meaning in your own words.

LESSON XVII.

Preparation for Composition.

Some animals that live in the sea are very useful to man. You must have studied about them in your Geographies. Tell what you have learned about, —

1. The Seal: where it lives; whether it breathes like a fish, or has lungs like a dog. What it feeds on. How it is caught. What is made from its skin. For what seal-oil is useful.

2. The Whale: where it lives; whether it breathes like fishes, or like land animals; whether its flesh is good to eat; what is made from its flesh, from its bones; in what part of the whale the most valuable bone is found; how the whale is caught.

LESSON XVIII.

Composition.

Write what you have learned about either the *seal* or the *whale*. Add some interesting story that you have read about the animal.

LESSON XIX.

Words frequently Misused.

Expect for *suspect, suppose,* or *presume.*

Whenever *expect* is correctly used it refers to *future time.* Remember this fact, and complete the following sentences with one of the words at the head of the lesson:

1. James's mother . . . . him to return at four P.M. to-morrow.
2. I . . . . that he has returned already, as I saw a valise in the hall.
3. You have not watered the plants for a week; I . . . . that they are all dead.
4. Was Charles late at school this morning? Oh! I . . . . so, he is almost always late.
5. I . . . . that Alice has finished the painting.

Use the words correctly in sentences of your own.

Plenty for *plentiful.*

The following sentences will show you the correct use of the two words:

We have had *plenty* of rain this summer.
The rain this summer has been *plentiful.*

Complete the following sentences:

1. Have you . . . . of money?
2. No, money is never . . . . with me.
3. Strawberries are cheap when they are . . . .
4. How . . . . the apples are this autumn!

Stop for *stay*, and *stopping* for *staying*.

To *stop* is to cease from motion.
To *stay* is to *remain*.
Complete the following sentences:

1. The train will .... at the station, and will .... there two hours.
2. George has been .... at his uncle's nearly all winter.
3. Do not .... on your way east, as you will want to .... with me a long time in Boston.

To the Teacher.—Ask frequently for a correct use of the words in such lessons as this. These lessons will be of little use, however, unless the errors in the ordinary speech of children are carefully corrected.

LESSON XX.

Conversation Exercise.

THE SUN AND MOON.

Where does the sun rise? Does it come above the horizon at the same point all the year round? Where does it set? Does it set at the same point on the horizon all the year round?

Is it directly over your head at noon? If not, is it north or south of you at that time? The point in the heavens directly over your head is called the *zenith*. During what month is the sun nearest the zenith at noon? During what month is it farthest from the zenith?

Does the moon rise and set? Does it rise at the same hour every night? What difference in the time of its rising have you noticed? Does the moon always appear to be of the same shape? What was its shape when you last saw it? The new moon,—its shape,—where first seen. The full moon,—its shape,—where first seen.

LESSON XXI.

Composition.

Write what you have learned of the sun and moon, making use, if you please, of the questions in Lesson XX.

To the Teacher. — In connection with your instruction in geography, call the attention of the pupils to the apparent motions of the heavenly bodies, to their size, distance, appearance, etc.

Lesson XX. furnishes material enough for several lessons, but for obvious reasons it has been thought best not to divide it.

LESSON XXII.

In the following beautiful poem, Mr. Whittier speaks of his friend, Henry W. Longfellow, who had recently died. Study it carefully and commit it to memory.

THE POET AND THE CHILDREN.

1. With the glory of winter sunshine
   Over his locks of gray,
   In the old historic mansion
   He sat on his last birthday,

2. With his books and his pleasant pictures
   And his household and his kin,
   While a sound as of myriads singing
   From far and near stole in.

3. It came from his own fair city,
   From the prairie's boundless plain,
   From the Golden Gate of sunset,
   From the cedar woods of Maine.

4. And his heart grew warm within him,
   And his moistening eyes grew dim,
   For he knew that his country's children
   Were singing the songs of him;

5. The lays of his life's glad morning,
   The psalms of his evening time,
   Whose echoes shall float forever
   On the winds of every clime.

6. All their beautiful consolations,
   Sent forth like birds of cheer,
   Came flocking back to his windows,
   And sang in the poet's ear.

7. Grateful, but solemn and tender,
   The music rose and fell
   With a joy akin to sadness,
   And a greeting like farewell.

8. With a sense of awe he listened
   To the voices sweet and young;
   The last of earth and the first of heaven
   Seemed in the songs they sung.

9. And, waiting a little longer
   For the wonderful change to come,
   He heard the Summoning Angel,
   Who calls God's children home;

10. And to him in a holier welcome
    Was the mystical meaning given
    Of the words of the blessed Master:
    "Of such is the kingdom of heaven."

To the Teacher. — The study of the foregoing poem should be made in connection with a knowledge of the circumstances which caused it to be written.

In addition to poems already suggested, read with the children, "Maud Muller," "The Pipes at Lucknow," selections from "Snow-Bound," "In School Days," "At Port Royal," "The Pumpkin," "Mabel Martin," and "The Sisters." See page 223.

CHAPTER TWELVE.

LESSON I.

Topics for Study and Conversation.

1. The home where Alice and Phœbe Cary were born. "Our Homestead."
2. Father, mother, and children.
3. Death of their mother, and the trials which followed. "An Order for a Picture."
4. How they obtained an education.
5. Their first efforts at writing. Subsequent success.
6. Going to New York, and the struggles that followed. "The Singer," by Whittier.
7. The home in New York.
8. Death and burial. "An Invalid's Plea." "Coming Home." "Nearer Home."
9. Life-long devotion of the two sisters for each other.
10. Other poems besides those mentioned above.

LESSON II.

Biographical Sketch.

Arrange notes, and write an account of the lives of Alice and Phœbe Cary. Mention as many of the writings of each as you have read, naming your favorite poem.

LESSON III.

Dictation Exercise.

The following extracts were taken from Alice Cary's poems:

1. The gifts that we have, heaven lends for right using,
   And not for ignoring, and not for abusing.

2. Not what we think, but what we do,
   Makes saints of us.

3. The day's last splendor fades and dies,
   And shadows one by one arise
   To light the candles of the skies.

4. Has not God planted every path with flowers
   Whose end is to be fair?

5. For he who is honest is noble,
   Whatever his fortunes or birth.

6. Fear often hath no whit of substance in it,
   And lives but just a minute.

7. Sunset! a hush is on the air,
   Their gray old heads the mountains bare
   As if the winds were saying prayer..

8. Thank God, when other power decays
And other pleasures die,
We still may set our dark to-days
In the light of days gone by.

To the Teacher.—Follow the dictation exercise with a conversation lesson.

LESSON IV.
Reproduction.

To the Teacher.—Read carefully with the children "The King's Jewel," by Phœbe Cary, and after a conversation exercise require the story to be written.

LESSON V.
Words often Mispronounced.

strength	singularly	bronchitis
violent	sovereign	juvenile
thanksgiving	pumpkin	reptile
Caucasian	menagerie	regularly

Preparation with Dictionary.

Copy the words, separating them into syllables, and mark the accented syllable in each word. Mark the vowel in each syllable so far as you can, and think how the word would sound if pronounced according to the marking.

1. What sound in the first word is liable to be substituted for that of *ng* ?
2. Sound the *vowels* in the second word.
3. Which syllable is accented in the third?
4. What sound has *a* in the accented syllable of the fourth?
5. Sound the vowels in the fifth.
6. What sound does *o* stand for in the sixth?
7. Always pronounce the seventh as it is spelled.

8. Pronounce the first syllable of the eighth; the second. What sound has *a*? For what sound does *g* stand?

9. What sound has *i* in the accented syllable of the ninth?

10. What sound has *i* in the tenth and eleventh?

11. Sound the vowels in the twelfth.

12. Pronounce the words with distinctness.

13. Define each word, or use it in a sentence.

14. Pronounce the words in Lesson V., Chapter Eleven.

LESSON VI.

A Letter.

Suppose your home to be in Ohio, but on account of ill health you have been traveling for several months in Mexico.

1. Make notes from which you can write a letter to your brother or sister at home, the letter to contain an account of the country, the products, the people, and their homes.

2. Add whatever you think will be of interest to your friends at home.

3. Write the letter in full.

To the Teacher. — Be sure that the pupils have obtained the necessary information before undertaking the letter-writing. The notes should be prepared as in previous lessons of this kind.

LESSON VII.

Review.

1. Of what use is *language?*
2. In what ways may we express our thoughts?
3. How does oral language differ from written?
4. What is a sentence?
5. Of what is a sentence composed?

LANGUAGE EXERCISES.

Uses of Words.
First *oral* and then *written*.

In the sentences below, tell for what purpose the words between the vertical lines are used.

Model.

Mary | wore | a pink | ribbon | in her hair. |
Mary is a word that tells us who wore the ribbon.
Wore is a word that tells us what Mary did.
Pink is a word that tells us the kind of ribbon.
Ribbon is a word that tells us what Mary wore.
In her hair is a group of words telling where Mary wore the ribbon.

1. John | saw | a cat | in the street. |
2. The soldiers | fought | bravely | in the battle. |
3. I | went | to church | one very cold day. |
4. The pupils | study | their | lessons | diligently. |
5. The young | lady | plays | the violin. |

To the Teacher. — Great care should be used in the selection of sentences, in order that the pupils may see the purpose for which the words are used. Uncommon uses of words, or peculiar expressions, should be avoided throughout this grade. Phrases and clauses should be taken entire.

LESSON VIII.
Dictation Exercise.

The following extracts were selected from Phœbe Cary's poems:

1. Hard indeed must a man be made
   By the toil and traffic of gain and trade,
   Who loves not the spot where a boy he played.

2. Life grows better every day
   If we live in deed and truth.

3. I ask not wealth, but power to take
And use the things I have aright;
Not years, but wisdom that shall make
My life a profit and delight.

4. All obedience worth the name
Must be prompt and ready.

5. And never since harvests were ripened
Or laborers born,
Have men gathered figs of thistles
Or grapes of the thorn.

6. All that's great and good is done
Just by patient trying.

7. Gaining victory from defeat,
That's the test that tries you.

To the Teacher. — A conversation exercise should follow the writing of the foregoing extracts. The dictation may be divided as desired.

LESSON IX.

Reproduction.

To the Teacher. — Read with the children, and make a careful study of, Alice Cary's poem, "An Order for a Picture." Bring vividly before the children, the scenes pictured in the poem, and make notes or topics for aids in their written reproduction.

LESSON X.

Verb-forms.

To the Teacher. — Assist the children, if necessary, in determining the correct forms of the following verbs, and in arranging them in a table as in Lesson XIV., Chapter Seven. To many children, some of the forms will be entirely new.

burst   forsake   show   fight   swim

LANGUAGE EXERCISES. 173

1. How many *different* forms of the first word do you find? of the fourth? the fifth?
2. Use in sentences the words that end with *n*.
3. Place *was* before each of the words in your fifth column. Use the words thus arranged, in sentences.
4. Name the derivatives for each word in Lesson XI., Chapter Eleven.
5. Use in sentences all the derivatives that you have just named ending in *n*.
6. Use in sentences, — *took, tore, threw, chose, wore.*

LESSON XI.

Conversation Exercise.

SUGAR-MAKING.

Maple-sugar, — where, and how made.

Sugar-making in Louisiana, — sugar-cane, — cutting, — crushing, — boiling, — molasses.

Is sugar made from any other sources than those mentioned?

Different kinds of sugar, — uses.

From what countries does most of our sugar come?

Are they cold, or warm, countries?

LESSON XII.

Composition on Sugar-Making.

Write what you have learned about sugar, adding, to the topics above, such others as seem to you important or interesting.

To the Teacher. — Such lessons as the foregoing are intended to suggest language-exercises in connection with the usual lessons in geography. Be sure that the pupils make a careful study of the whole subject before they attempt to write upon it. As has been said many times before in this book, *an oral lesson should always precede the written.*

174   LANGUAGE EXERCISES.

LESSON XIII.

Conversation Exercise.

PLANTS.

For what are the plants named below useful?

wheat	potatoes	dates	flax
rice	oranges	corn	grapes
grass	lemons	tobacco	coffee

To the Teacher.—Some of the plants named above are useful in two or three ways. Be sure that these receive attention in the conversation exercise. Some of the topics may be assigned for study with a view to composition writing. In case this is done, topics for study should be placed on the blackboard, and the composition should follow the order of the topics.

LESSON XIV.

Exercise in Articulation.

Speak the following combinations of words, carefully separating the words in each combination:

won't you	did you	did n't you
can't you	could you	could n't you
don't you	would you	would n't you
must you	had you	had n't you

To the Teacher.—Frequent drill on these combinations of words will be very useful. They should at first be spoken slowly, so that the articulation may be perfect, and then more rapidly.

Review.

Pronounce distinctly the words given in the pronunciation exercises of Parts I. and II.

LESSON XV.

Oral Paraphrase.

The following stanzas were selected from Alice Cary's poems. Tell their meaning in your own words.

1. A good many workers I've known in my time,
   Some builders of houses, some builders of rhyme;
   And they that were prospered, were prospered, I know,
   By the intent and the meaning of "Hoe your own row."
   From "Old Maxims."

2. To conscience be true, and to man true,
   Keep faith, hope, and love in your breast,
   And when you have done all you can do,
   Why, then, you may trust for the rest.
   From "A Sermon for Young Folks."

3. So, boy, if you want to be sure of your bread
   Ere the good time of working is gone,
   Brush the cobwebs of nonsense all out of your head,
   And take up your hoe, and move on.
   From "Waiting for Something to Turn Up."

4. To know the beauty of cleanness
   The heart must be clean and sweet;
   We must love our neighbor to get his love, —
   As we measure he will mete.
   From "Best to the Best."

5. Look for goodness, look for gladness,
   You will meet them all the while;
   If you bring a smiling visage
   To the glass, you meet a smile.
   From "A Fragment."

To the Teacher. — See notes of direction on similar lessons in the two chapters next preceding this.

LESSON XVII.
Information Exercise.

To the Teacher. — Read with the children the following account of the snail, and make it the subject of conversation. For a second lesson, prepare notes, and then require the pupils to write an orderly description of the snail. This exercise should be given during the season when it will be possible to obtain the shells from brooks or ditches.

Before studying the following description of a snail, find if possible a live specimen in some brook in the neighborhood. As you study the description, compare it with the snail which you have found, and you may learn much that is new to you as well as interesting.

LIVE SHELLS.

Here is a shell with the *animal* inside. I found it under a lily-pad. It is a water-snail. We can see, across the aperture, a kind of broad *foot*. The animal moves about by means of this foot. If we watch, we shall see two little feelers stretched out from under the shell. These are called *tentacles*, and the snail uses them to feel its way along. It has *eyes*, too, — two little black dots, at the base of the tentacles. The *mouth* is between the tentacles, and we might have seen where the snail had made its dinner from the side of the lily-pad. The part of the snail that has the tentacles, eyes, and mouth is called the head.

The other end of the snail is fastened to the inside of the shell; so it must carry its shell on its back when it travels on the lily-pads. It is well that it cannot leave the shell at home, for this is its only protection from an enemy. The snail breathes air just as we do. If you could put this snail into water and watch it, you would soon see it coming up to the surface. It brings one edge of the aperture to the water's edge; then a little hole opens in its side, and the air goes into the lung.

LESSON XVIII.

A Letter.

Write a letter from the city of Washington, giving such information as you have gained at school, from books and papers at home, or from conversation with those who have visited the city.

Topics for Study and Conversation.

1. The founding of the city. 2. Location, and why named Washington. 3. Plan of the city. 4. Public buildings. 5. A description of the Capitol and the White House. 6. An account of the President's Reception.

LESSON XIX.

Oral Paraphrase.

The following stanzas were selected from Phœbe Cary's poems:

1. Wherever you stay or wherever you roam,
    In the days while you live in clover,
  You should gather your honey and bring it home,
  Because the winter will surely come
    When the summer of life is over.
              From "Hives and Homes."

2. May you never, never have to say
  When a wave from the past on some dreary day
    Its wrecks at your feet is strewing,
  "My father had not been bowed so low,
  Nor my mother left me long ago,
    But for deeds of my misdoing."
              From "To the Children."

3. Do you suppose a book can tell
Maxims of prudence, half so well
As the little ant, who is telling
To man, as she patiently goes and comes,
Bearing her precious grains and crumbs,
How want is kept from the dwelling?
From " Easy Lessons."

4. Whatever a story can teach to you
Of the good a little thing may do,
The hidden brook is showing,
Whose quiet way is only seen
Because of its banks, so fresh and green,
And the flowers beside it growing.
From " Easy Lessons."

LESSON XX.

Words expressing Color, Size, and Form.

1. Write, in a column, a list of ten words that may be used in describing the color of objects; as, *red, buff*, etc.

2. After each word in the list, write the name of an appropriate object; as, A red rose.

3. Use the ten groups of words in thoughtful sentences; as, A *red* rose could be seen in a tiny vase on the shelf.

4. Write a list of ten words which are names of familiar objects. With each of these words connect two others, one of which expresses *size* and the other *form;* as, An *immense, flat* plain stretched far away towards the north.

To the Teacher. — Review this lesson frequently until the pupils become skillful in connecting nouns with appropriate adjectives; then the pupils may use three adjectives (size, form, color) with one noun, and afterward expand the group into a sentence.

LESSON XX.

Study and commit to memory the following beautiful poem by Alice Cary:

WORK.

1. Down and up, and up and down,
    Over and over and over;
   Turn in the little seed, dry and brown,
    Turn out the bright red clover.
   Work, and the sun your work will share,
    And the rain in its time will fall;
   For Nature, she worketh every-where,
    And the grace of God through all.

2. With hand on the spade, and heart in the sky,
    Dress the ground and till it;
   Turn in the little seed, brown and dry,
    Turn out the golden millet.
   Work, and your house shall be duly fed;
    Work, and rest shall be won;
   I hold that a man had better be dead
    Than alive, when his work is done.

3. Down and up, and up and down,
    On the hill-top, low in the valley;
   Turn in the little seed, dry and brown,
    Turn out the rose and lily.
   Work with a plan, or without a plan,
    And your ends they shall be shaped true;
   Work, and learn at first hand, like a man,—
    The best way to *know* is to *do*.

4. Down and up till life shall close,
   Ceasing not your praises;
   Turn in the mild white winter snows,
   Turn out the sweet spring daisies.
   Work, and the sun your work will share,
   And the rain in its time will fall;
   For Nature, she worketh every-where,
   And the grace of God through all.

          ALICE CARY.

To the Teacher.—Make a careful study of this beautiful poem; you can do nothing better than to impress its fine sentiment. In connection with this study, read the poem, "Idle," by the same author. In addition to Alice Cary's poems, already suggested in this book, read with the children "The Gray Swan," "A Fable of Cloud-Land," "Faded Leaves," and "The Cradle Song." See page 223.

In addition to the poems of Phœbe Cary which have been named already, read "The Hero of Fort Wagner," and "Ready."

LANGUAGE EXERCISES. 181

Oliver Wendell Holmes.

CHAPTER THIRTEEN.

LESSON I.

Topics for Study and Conversation.

1. Birthplace and family of Oliver Wendell Holmes.
2. Early home and school life.

3. College life and famous classmates.
4. Studies of law and medicine.
5. Professorships.
6. A doctor in Boston, — long practice.
7. Travels in Europe.
8. His writings.
9. His own family.
10. His age.

LESSON II.
Biographical Sketch.

Write, in an orderly manner, what you have learned about Dr. Oliver Wendell Holmes.

Divide your composition into the proper number of paragraphs.

LESSON III.
Dictation Exercise.

The following extracts were selected from Holmes's poems:

1. The flowering moments of the mind
   Drop half their petals in our speech.

2. Day hath put on his jacket, and around
   His burning bosom hath buttoned it with stars.

3. On all her boughs the stately chestnut cleaves
   The gummy shroud that wraps her embryo leaves.

4. The crack-brained bobolink courts his crazy mate
   Poised on a bulrush tipsy with his weight.

5. The sweetest of smiles is the smile when we part,
   When the light round the lips is a ray from the heart.

6. The outward forms the inner man reveal, —
   We guess the pulp before we cut the peel.

7. Be firm! one constant element in luck
Is genuine, solid, old Teutonic pluck.

8. And with new notions, — let me change the rule, —
Don't strike the iron till it's slightly cool.

To the Teacher. — Follow the dictation with a conversation exercise on the meaning of the extracts.

LESSON IV.

Business Letters.

Business letters differ somewhat from other letters, both in form and in contents. The address of such letters is more formal, and the contents refer only to matters of real business. All matters relating to social or domestic affairs should generally be excluded. A business letter should be clear and concise, without unnecessary preliminary remarks or uncalled-for explanations. No more words should be used than are necessary · nor should any essential words be omitted.

These letters require the same careful attention to details as do other letters. The address on the envelope should be plainly written, and the writer's own address may be printed on the upper left-hand corner.

Business letters include letters of introduction, letters of application, letters of recommendation, mercantile letters, etc.

Oral.

1. How do business letters differ from other letters?
2. What is meant by the "address" of a letter?
3. What are "social" and "domestic" affairs?
4. Give the meaning of the following words, and use them in sentences of your own: — *excluded, concise, preliminary, details.*

5. Mention the different kinds of business letters, and explain what you understand by each kind.

LESSON V.

Dictation Exercise.

John D. Wilson, Esq., Boston, Mass.

Dear Sir, — Allow me to introduce to you the bearer, Mr. Thomas Williams, a graduate of Harvard University, who visits your city for the purpose of finding employment in connection with some daily newspaper.

He is a young man of excellent character and superior ability. Any assistance you may render him I shall esteem as a personal favor.

Yours very truly,

CHAS. W. HARPER.

You have a schoolmate who wishes to secure a place as clerk in a store. Write a letter, introducing him to some business man with whom you are acquainted.

LESSON VI.

Words often Mispronounced.

forgetting	dishonest	whether
immediately	grasses	robust
magazine	fairies	Chinese
Jerusalem	excursion	considerable

Make careful preparation of this lesson, — in spelling, pronunciation, and use of words, as suggested in Lesson V., Chapter Twelve.

1. In the first word, what sound has *e?* Sound *ng*.

2. How many syllables in the second? Sound the vowel in each syllable?

LANGUAGE EXERCISES. 185

3. Which syllable is accented in the third?
4. Sound the vowels in the fourth; few people speak the word correctly.
5. What sound has the first *s* in the fifth?
6. In the sixth and seventh, sound the *a*.
7. In the eighth, sound the third syllable.
8. What is the first sound in the ninth?
9. In the tenth, which syllable is accented?
10. Sound the *s* in the eleventh.
11. How many syllables in the twelfth?
12. Pronounce the words distinctly.
13. Name the derivatives, and give the root-word of each.
14. Use the words in sentences.
15. Pronounce the words in Lesson V., Chapter Twelve.

LESSON VII.

Information Exercise.

FROGS.

Frogs lay their eggs in the water. Before the egg is many days old, it is hatched, and out comes an odd little thing with a large head, a long flat tail, and no body at all. This is called a tadpole. For a few days it has a tuft of soft pink threads on each side of its head. These are the gills, which enable the tadpole to breathe in the water. It lives the life of a fish, and finds all its food in the water. But soon a wonderful change takes place; its gills disappear, and lungs form in the chest. After this it can no longer breathe in the water, but must rise to the surface for air.

Four legs gradually grow out, and at the same time the tail disappears. The animal is now a perfect frog, and spends its time partly on land and partly in the water. In winter it crawls into a hole and sleeps there until spring.

A frog may produce a thousand eggs in a year, but scarcely one egg in the thousand produces a young one that lives to reach its winter retreat.

Conversation Exercise.
Topics for Study and Conversation.

1. Eggs, — where laid; color, size.
2. Tadpoles, — description, gills, head, tail.
3. Describe the changes that take place.
4. How the frog swims, — how it catches its food.
5. Winter quarters.

To the Teacher. — Lessons in Natural History are of little value if unaccompanied by observation. When schools are so situated that pupils are unable to obtain specimens for examination, pictures or blackboard drawings may be made very helpful.

LESSON VIII.
Composition.

Write what you have learned about the frog, dividing your composition into five paragraphs.

LESSON IX.
Synonyms.

1. Select, and arrange in sets of three each, the synonyms in the following list. See Lesson X., Chapter Eleven.

smell	uncommon	impertinent	sport
endure	real	odor	saucy
scarce	seem	suffer	true
aid	rude	rare	look
scent	play	assist	appear
help	bear	genuine	pastime

LANGUAGE EXERCISES. 187

2. Study the words that are synonymous, and find out, if possible, how they differ in meaning.

3. Use the synonyms that differ in meaning in such a way as to show the difference.

LESSON X.

Dictation Exercise.

MAXIMS AND PROVERBS.

1. Keep your shop and your shop will keep you.
2. If at first you don't succeed, try, try again.
3. Least said, soonest mended.
4. Little pitchers have large ears.
5. One swallow does not make a summer.
6. Rome was not built in a day.
7. Silks and satins put out the kitchen fire.
8. Too many cooks spoil the broth.
9. Discretion is the better part of valor.
10. A barking dog never bites.
11. Lazy folks take the most pains.
12. Laziness travels so slowly that poverty soon overtakes it.

To the Teacher. — After the writing of this lesson and its correction, a conversation exercise will follow, of course. Ask for any incident or experience which proves the truth of any one of the proverbs.

LESSON XI.

Neighborhood Study.

Topics for Conversation.

1. Places one mile distant from your school-house; two miles; five miles; ten miles.
2. Public conveyances, — stages, horse-cars, steam-cars.
3. Parts of the neighborhood that are level, hilly, mountainous.

LANGUAGE EXERCISES.

4. Water in the vicinity, — brooks, rivers, ponds, lakes, and with what other waters they are connected.

To the Teacher.— This and similar lessons may be followed by a written composition.

LESSON XII.

Oral Paraphrase or Conversation.

The following stanzas were selected from Holmes's poems:

1. Slowly the mist o'er the meadow was creeping,
   Bright on the dewy buds glistened the sun,
   When from his couch, while his children were sleeping,
   Rose the bold rebel and shouldered his gun.
   From "Lexington."

2. The sun stepped down from his golden throne,
   And lay in the silent sea,
   And the lily had folded her satin leaves,
   For a sleepy thing was she;
   What is the lily dreaming of?
   Why crisp the waters blue?
   See, see, she has lifted her varnished lid!
   Her white leaves are glistening through.
   From "The Star and the Lily."

3. Welcome to the day returning,
   Dearer still as ages flow,
   While the torch of faith is burning
   Long as Freedom's altars glow!
   See the hero whom it gave us,
   Slumbering on a mother's breast;
   For the arm he stretched to save us,
   Be its morn forever blest!
   From "Ode for Washington's Birthday."

4. This is the ship of pearl, which poets feign
Sails the unshadowed main, —
The venturous bark that flings
On the sweet summer wind its purpled wings
In gulfs enchanted, where the siren sings,
And coral reefs lie bare,
Where the cold sea-maids rise to sun their streaming hair."
From "The Chambered Nautilus."

To the Teacher. — See notes on similar lessons in preceding chapters.

LESSON XIII.

Review.

Review Lessons I. and II., Chapter Six.

When direct quotations are complete statements they should begin with capital letters; but if the quotation is an incomplete statement, the capital is frequently omitted.

It is usual to make complete paragraphs of long quotations from books or letters.

Double marks are generally used for a quotation; but single marks (' ') are used when one quotation occurs within another.

Dictation Exercise.

1. It has been well said, "The tongue is a little member and boasteth great things."

2. "The question now is," said he, "how shall we know what are good books?"

3. Whittier's story, "The Rattlesnake Hunter," is based upon fact.

4. "Be ready to come when I call you," said his mother.

5. In the preceding sentence, the words "said his mother," should not be enclosed by quotation marks.

6. "On one occasion," says Whittier, "I was told that a foreigner had applied to my mother for lodging. 'What if a son of mine were in a strange land?' she said to herself."

Notice that the quotations are separated from the rest of the sentence by marks of punctuation.

LESSON XIV.

Preparation for Letter-Writing,

Topics for Conversation.

1. What is the longest or the most interesting journey you ever made?
2. How did you go? Describe the route.
3. Did you meet any pleasant people on the way? Did you meet any who were not pleasant? Tell all about them.
4. If you met with any accident, or had any trouble about your baggage, describe it.
5. Describe the country through which you passed. Was it level or hilly? Did you see any mountains? any rivers? If so, describe them.
6. What did you observe that made you think the people were prosperous, or otherwise?

To the Teacher.—These "journeys" may be purely imaginary; but if so, a conversation exercise should precede the written work, and suggestive notes should be placed on the blackboard to assist the pupils.

LESSON XV.

Letter.

Write a letter to your teacher from such topics in Lesson XIV. as you think would be most interesting.

LANGUAGE EXERCISES. 191

Combine with this account such descriptions of persons and places as will give a pleasant variety to your letter. Draw and direct the envelope.

To the Teacher. — Allow the pupils occasionally to enclose their letters in real envelopes, and to direct and deliver them.

LESSON XVI.

Verb-forms.

The correct use of the following words is as difficult as anything that children have to learn in English. The boy or girl who is willing to give them close thought and careful use can conquer them within a few days.

sit	sits	sitting	sat	sat
set	sets	setting	set	set
lie	lies	lying	lay	lain
lay	lays	laying	laid	laid

To the Teacher. — Require much oral practice in the use of these words to describe actions seen in the school-room, and review the lesson frequently. After oral drill, give written exercises similar to the following: —

Complete the following sentences with words chosen from the table above:

1. I .... the pointer on the table. It is .... there now.
2. .... the chair on the floor, and .... down in it. I am .... in it, and have .... here an hour.
3. Charles is .... his overcoat on my desk. I am willing that it should .... there.
4. Mary .... in bed this morning until eight o'clock. If she had .... there much longer she would have missed her breakfast.
5. Where does the snow .... on the ground all the year?

6. I have .... still five minutes; I can not .... still any longer.

7. The dog is .... near the fire.

8. The baby .... her head on the dog, and there she .... now fast asleep.

LESSON XVII.
Dictation Exercise.

BOSTON, Nov. 19, 1888.

Messrs. Jordan, Marsh & Co.

Gentlemen, — I learn from an advertisement in the *Transcript* that you are in want of an assistant book-keeper. Having had considerable experience as book-keeper in a large house in New York, I beg leave to offer myself to you for the position.

I am able to show you papers from my late employers, vouching for my ability and for my integrity. Will you be so kind as to name a time when I may venture to ask a personal interview?

Very respectfully yours,

MADISON K. BARTLETT.

Write an application for employment to some business man in the neighborhood. State your qualifications and give references.

LESSON XVIII.
Uses of Words.
First *oral* and then *written*.

Tell the uses of the words between the vertical lines in the following sentences. See Lesson VII., Chapter Twelve.

1. The cargo | was | thrown | overboard | during the storm. |

2. Professor Miles | gave | an excellent | lesson | in geography. |

3. The boy | who always tells the truth, | will be loved | by all. |
4. I | saw | the man | who fell from the third-story window. |
5. The teacher | selected | the slate | which was on John's desk. |
6. Mary | told | me | that she was going home. |
7. The knife | which you gave me | lies | on the desk. |
8. The letter | that you wrote | last | Wednesday | reached | me | to-day. |

To the Teacher. — After the pupils have learned what clauses are used for *as wholes*, they may be required to tell the use of words selected from them.

LESSON XIX.

Reproduction.

To the Teacher. — Read with the children Holmes's "Ballad of the Boston Tea-Party." Tell them about the "Old South" meeting-house, and the famous meeting held there just before the "party." Tell them about the "Indians," who they really were, and what they did.

For a second lesson, make notes, and have a written account of the incident and the poem.

LESSON XX.

Homonyms.

Opposite each of the following words, write its homonym:

eight	bade	dyeing ....
plain	berth	feat ....
pour	ceiling	guilt ....
assent	draught	hale ....

1. Define the given words or use them in sentences

2. Define the words you have supplied, or use them in sentences.

3. Define or use in sentences the words given in Lesson XV., Chapter Eleven.

LESSON XXI.

Study and commit to memory the following poem, by Oliver Wendell Holmes. It should be an inspiration to boys and girls.

UNION AND LIBERTY.

1. Flag of the heroes who left us their glory,
 Borne through their battle-fields' thunder and flame,
 Blazoned in song and illumined in story,
 Wave o'er us all who inherit their fame!
 CHORUS: Up with our banner bright,
 Sprinkled with starry light,
 Spread its fair emblems from mountain to shore,
 While through the sounding sky,
 Loud rings the Nation's cry,—
 UNION AND LIBERTY! ONE EVERMORE!

2. Light of our firmament, guide of our Nation,
 Pride of her children, and honored afar,
 Let the wide beams of thy full constellation
 Scatter each cloud that would darken a star!
 CHORUS:—

3. Empire unsceptered! what foe shall assail thee,
 Bearing the standard of Liberty's van?
 Think not the God of thy fathers shall fail thee,
 Striving with men for the birthright of man.
 CHORUS:—

LANGUAGE EXERCISES.

4. Yet if, by madness and treachery blighted,
   Dawns the dark hour when the sword thou must draw,
   Then with the arms of thy millions united,
   Smite the bold traitors to Freedom and Law!
   CHORUS:—

5. Lord of the Universe! shield us and guide us,
   Trusting Thee always, through shadow and sun!
   Thou hast united us, who shall divide us?
   Keep us, O keep us the MANY IN ONE.
   CHORUS:—

To the Teacher.—A poem so full of noble patriotism as the foregoing is worthy of careful study and thought. A spirited exercise may be conducted by having the several stanzas recited by single pupils, and the chorus in a rousing manner by the entire school.

Holmes's poem, "A Hymn of Peace," may well be sung to Keller's "American Hymn" by every school-boy and girl in America.

In addition to the poems suggested in Chapter Nine, read with the children, and talk about, "The Dorchester Giant," "Dorothy Q," "God Save the Flag," "The Last Leaf," "Old Ironsides," and "The Comet." See page 223.

196 LANGUAGE EXERCISES.

CHAPTER FOURTEEN.

LESSON I.

Topics for Study and Conversation.

1. Birthplace and home circle of James Russell Lowell.
2. School life.
3. College life.
4. Law studies. Why he left the law.
5. Editor of the *Atlantic Monthly*.

LANGUAGE EXERCISES. 197

6. Professor at Harvard University.
7. Minister to Spain and to Great·Britain.
8. His own home at "Elmwood," and his family. Longfellow's poem, "The Two Angels."
9. Some of Lowell's poems.

LESSON II.

Biographical Sketch.

Write a sketch of the life and writings of James Russell Lowell, using some or all of the topics in Lesson I. This work will be much easier if, before writing, you make full notes of your study of the topics in the previous lesson.

LESSON III.

Dictation and Conversation Exercise.

The following extracts were selected from Lowell's poems:

1. A little of thy steadfastness
 Rounded with leafy gracefulness,
   Old oak, give me.

2. Glorious fountain! Let my heart be
 Fresh, changeful, constant, upward, like thee.

3. 'Tis heaven alone that is given away,
 'Tis only God may be had for the asking.

4. Life is a leaf of paper white
 Whereon each of us may write
 His word or two, and then comes night.

5. The Holy Supper is kept indeed
 In whatso we share with another's need.

6. He's true to God, who's true to man.

7. How strange are the freaks of memory!
The lessons of life we forget,
While a trifle, a trick of color,
In the wonderful web we set.

8. The maple puts her corals on in May,
While loitering frosts about the lowlands cling.

LESSON IV.

Reproduction.

To the Teacher. — Read with the children Lowell's poem, "The Singing Leaves." A good understanding of the poem may require two or three readings, which should of course be accompanied with conversation and explanation. Require the pupils to include one or more extracts from the poem in the written reproduction of the story.

LESSON V.

Dictation Exercise.

INFORMAL NOTE OF INVITATION.

My Dear Harry, —

Next Wednesday will be my birthday, and I propose to invite a few choice friends to celebrate the event with me in the evening. Will you come?

Yours sincerely,

JOE.

4417 Rose Av., Chicago.

FORMAL NOTE OF INVITATION.

Mrs. Henry B. Wallace requests the pleasure of Mr. and Mrs. A. P. Stuart's company, Wednesday, June 16, from seven to ten o'clock.

245 Forest Av., Cambridge.

1. Write an informal note of invitation to some friend to dine with you at five o'clock next Wednesday afternoon.

2. Write a formal note of invitation to some acquaintance to attend a concert with you next Thursday evening.

LESSON VI.

Neighborhood Study.

Topics for Study and Conversation.

1. Soil, — loam, sand, gravel, clay; which are found on the surface; which underneath. Some of the uses of the different kinds of soil.

2. Rocks, — where found; different kinds; uses.

3. Are there any mines of coal or iron in the neighborhood? Any quarries of stone? Uses of the different minerals.

4. Animals, wild and domestic. Uses of these animals.

To the Teacher. — Such lessons as the preceding require close observation on the part of the pupils, but it should be under the direction of the teacher. The *habit* of observation cannot be too carefully formed.

LESSON VII.

Notes of Invitation, etc.

1. Your birthday comes soon, and your mother has promised you a birthday party. Write a note of invitation to some friend whom you wish to be present.

2. Write an answer accepting the invitation.

3. Write an answer giving a reason for declining.

4. You have received, by express, from your uncle a beautiful Christmas-box containing several things that you have long wanted. Write a letter of thanks.

LESSON VIII.

Who and Which.

Rewrite the following sentences, inserting *who* or *which*, and such other words as may be necessary, after each italicized word.

Model.

The *tree* is one hundred years old.
The tree which stands on the corner is one hundred years old.

1. It was *General Grant.*
2. My *friend* is now in New York.
3. This *lesson* is very difficult.
4. The *boy* will become a good man.
5. I cut down the *tree.*
6. The dog caught the *rabbit.*
7. The *dog* caught the rabbit.
8. The *dog* caught the *rabbit.*

Complete the following sentences:

1. My older brother whom . . . .
2. I saw the old man to whom . . . .
3. Have you seen the girl whom . . . .

LESSON IX.

Study and commit to memory the following stanzas selected from one of Lowell's poems:

SUMMER.

1. What is so rare as a day in June?
    Then, if ever, come perfect days;
  Then Heaven tries the earth if it be in tune,
    And over it softly her warm ear lays.

Whether we look or whether we listen,
We hear life murmur or see it glisten;
Every clod feels a stir of might,
An instinct within it which reaches and towers,
And, groping blindly above it for light,
Climbs to a soul in grass and flowers.

2. The flush of life may well be seen
Thrilling back over hills and valleys;
The cowslip startles in meadows green,
The buttercup catches the sun in its chalice,
And there's never a leaf nor a blade too mean
To be some happy creature's palace.

3. The little bird sits at his door in the sun
Atilt like a blossom among the leaves,
And lets his illumined being o'errun
With the deluge of summer it receives;
His mate feels the eggs beneath her wings,
And the heart in her dumb breast flutters and sings;
He sings to the wide world and she to her nest;—
In the nice ear of nature, which song is the best?

4. The breeze comes whispering in our ear,
That dandelions are blossoming near,
That maize has sprouted, that streams are flowing,
That the river is bluer than the sky,
That the robin is plastering his home hard by;
And if the breeze kept the good news back,
For other couriers we should not lack;
We could guess it all by yon heifer's lowing,—
And hark! how clear bold chanticleer,
Warmed with the new wine of the year,
Tells all in his lusty crowing!

From "The Vision of Sir Launfal."

LESSON X.

Words often Mispronounced.

admirable	architect	envelop
area	alpaca	envelope
avalanche	archipelago	exquisite
barbarous	Caribbean	granary

After careful preparation with the Dictionary, answer the following questions:

1. In the first word, which syllable is accented? What is the root-word?
2. Which syllable is accented in the second? Sound the vowels, and name the vowel sounds.
3. In the third, what sound has *ch?* Which syllable is accented? Sound *a* in the accented syllable.
4. Sound each syllable in the fourth.
5. Sound *ch* in the fifth. Sound the first syllable. Sound the last syllable. Sound the *i*.
6. How many syllables in the sixth?
7. Sound each vowel in the seventh. Sound *ch*.
8. Which is the accented syllable in the eighth? Notice the spelling.
9. See how much you can find out about the ninth and tenth.
10. Which syllable are you to accent in the eleventh? Be sure to do so.
11. What sound has *a* in the accented syllable of the twelfth? What is the root of the twelfth?
12. After the words have been pronounced, write them, separating each into syllables and marking the accent.
13. Define the words or use them in oral sentences.

LESSON XI.

Letter from Florida.

Assume that you were an invalid, and went to Florida in December. You improved rapidly in health, so that you were able to spend most of your time very pleasantly out-of-doors. In April you wrote a letter from Florida, to a friend in your native State, from the topics below.
Reproduce the letter in full.

1. Reasons for going to Florida.
2. The climate there in winter.
3. Vegetation and fruits.
4. How the time was spent.
5. You expect to return in May, and you speak of the contrast that will appear.

LESSON XII.

Uses of Words.

First *oral* and then *written*.

Tell the use of the words and phrases between the vertical lines in the following selection:

Nail | to the mast | her | holy | flag, |
Set | every | threadbare | sail, |
And give | her | to the god | of storms, |
The lightning | and | the gale! |

1. Which words in the selection are nouns?
2. Which nouns are singular?
3. Which nouns are plural?
4. Use each noun in the opposite number?
5. Review Lessons XII. and XIII. in Chapter Three.

LESSON XIII.

Dictation Exercise.

PROVERBS.

1. Never judge a book by its cover.
2. Wisdom is better than rubies.
3. A wise son maketh a glad father.
4. He that is surety for a stranger shall smart for it.
5. The way of the transgressor is hard.
6. A soft answer turneth away wrath.
7. A merry heart maketh a cheerful countenance.
8. Wine is a mocker; strong drink is raging.
9. Doing nothing is doing ill.
10. Never make a mountain out of a mole-hill.
11. Every fool will be meddling.
12. A good name is rather to be chosen than great riches.
13. He is a poor workman that quarrels with his tools.
14. United we stand, divided we fall.

To the Teacher. — If possible, secure the writing of each sentence from a single reading. An occasional caution will secure correct capitals and punctuation.

No material could be better for a conversation exercise than that in the foregoing lesson.

LESSON XIV.

Business Letters.

1. Write a letter of recommendation for a personal friend.
2. Write an application for a position as teacher in a neighboring town.
3. Write a note of thanks for some favor received.
4. Write to a friend, extending an invitation to dine with you.

LESSON XV.
Words often Misused.
Some for *somewhat.*

The following sentences indicate the correct use of the words in italics:

Some of the boys are *very* noisy to-day.
My father is *somewhat* better this morning.

Complete the following sentences:

You came to church . . . . late last Sunday.
Is that boy tired? No, but he is . . . . lazy.

Quantity for *number.*

We should use *number* in speaking of things that may be counted; as, a *number* of sheep, a *number* of cattle. We say, a *quantity* of oats, a *quantity* of hay.

1. Use the word *number* in three different sentences.
2. Use *quantity* in three different sentences.

Only.

The difficulty in using *only* arises from not knowing where to place it in a sentence.

Notice and explain the different meanings conveyed by the word *only* in the following sentences:

1. *Only* the boy snatched the apple.
2. The boy *only* snatched the apple.
3. The boy snatched *only* the apple.

In the following sentences use *only* in as many different places as possible, and explain the changes in meaning:

1. My sister read the Bible this morning.
2. Little George hit his brother in the eye.
3. Boys and girls whisper in school.

LESSON XVI.

Oral Paraphrase or Conversation.

The following choice stanzas were selected from Lowell's poems:

1. O poor man's son! scorn not thy state;
   There is worse weariness than thine,
   In merely being rich and great.
   Toil only gives the soul to shine
   And makes rest fragrant and benign;
   A heritage, it seems to me,
   Worth being poor to hold in fee.
                    From "The Heritage."

2. Let fraud and wrong and baseness shiver,
   For still between them and the sky
   The falcon, Truth, hangs poised forever,
   And marks them with his vengeful eye.
                    From "The Falcon."

3. They are slaves who fear to speak
   For the fallen and the weak;
   They are slaves who will not choose
   Hatred, scoffing, and abuse,
   Rather than in silence shrink
   From the truth they needs must think;
   They are slaves who dare not be
   In the right with two or three.
                    From "Stanzas on Freedom."

4. Ah! let us hope that to our praise
   Good God not only reckons
   The moments when we tread his ways,
   But when the spirit beckons,—

That some slight good is also wrought
Beyond self-satisfaction,
When we are simply good in thought,
Howe'er we fail in action.
From "Longing."

LESSON XVII.

Classification.

Make a list of things that are —

sweet	salt	oily	delicious
acid	spicy	sour	fragrant
bitter	crisp	tart	poisonous

Name several things which are made from the following materials:

glass	cloth	tin	lime
wood	paper	lead	flour
iron	wool	horn	steel

To the Teacher.—The answers should be well-constructed sentences.

LESSON XVIII.

Classification (*Continued*).

You have already learned to classify things as animal, vegetable, or mineral. A horse is an animal, a potato is a vegetable, and a stone is a mineral. Some things grow; as trees, fruits, flowers, etc. These are called *natural* products. Some things are made by hand or by machinery; as boots, furniture, pictures, etc. Such things are *manufactured* products.

1. In the second list in Lesson XVII., which things are natural products and which are manufactured?

2. Select the manufactured products from the list, and tell *of what* and *how* they are made.

LESSON XIX.

Preparation for Composition.

COAL.

Topics for Study and Conversation.

1. Different kinds of coal.
2. Coal-mining.
3. Anthracite and bituminous coal,—how do they differ? In what parts of the country are they found?
4. Franklin coal,—cannel coal; why so called?
5. When coal was first used for fuel.
6. Gas manufactured from coal. Coke.
7. Charcoal,—how made,—its use.

LESSON XX.

Composition.

Write what you have learned about coal, using the topics in Lesson XIX. in the order given.

LESSON XXI.

Study and commit to memory the following stanzas selected from one of Lowell's poems:

WINTER.

1. Down swept the chill wind from the mountain peak,
   From the snow five thousand summers old;
   On open world and hill-top bleak
   It had gathered all the cold,
   And whirled it like sleet on the wanderer's cheek;
   It carried a shiver everywhere
   From the unleafed boughs and the pastures bare;

2. The little brook heard it, and built a roof
   'Neath which he could house him winter-proof.
   All night by the white star's frosty gleams
   He groined his arches and matched his beams;

Slender and clear were his crystal spars
As the lashes of light that trim the stars;

3. He sculptured every summer delight
In his halls and chambers out of sight;
Sometimes his tinkling waters slipt
Down through a frost-leaved forest crypt,
Long, sparkling aisles of steel-stemmed trees
Bending to counterfeit a breeze.

4. Sometimes the roof no fretwork knew
But silvery mosses that downward grew;
Sometimes it was carved in sharp relief
With quaint arabesques of ice-fern leaf;
Sometimes it was simply smooth and clear
For the gladness of heaven to shine through, and here
He had caught the nodding bulrush-tops
And hung them thickly with diamond drops
That crystalled the beams of moon and sun
And made a diamond of every one.

5. No mortal builder's most rare device
Could match this winter-palace of ice.
'Twas as if every image that mirrored lay
In his depths serene through the summer day,
Each fleeting shadow of earth and sky,
Lest the happy model should be lost,
Had been mimicked in fairy masonry
By the elfin builders of the frost.

From "The Vision of Sir Launfal."

To the Teacher.—It is hoped that the teacher will read with the pupils the whole of "The Vision of Sir Launfal." The poem has no superior, whether we consider beauty of expression or the lesson taught. See note at the close of Chapter Five.

210   LANGUAGE EXERCISES.

CHAPTER FIFTEEN.

LESSON I.

Topics for Study and Conversation.

1. Birthplace and home circle of William Cullen Bryant.
2. Boyhood.
3. School life. Wonderful progress.
4. Short college life, and reasons therefor.

LANGUAGE EXERCISES. 211

5. Early writings.
6. Professional studies.
7. Editorial work.
8. His travels.
9. His homes.
10. His death and burial. His age.

LESSON II.

Biographical Sketch.

Make notes of your study of the topics in Lesson I., and then write an account of the life and writings of Mr. Bryant. Divide your composition into paragraphs.

LESSON III.

Dictation Exercise.

The following verses were selected from Bryant's poems. Study them carefully, and find out their meaning.

1. The groves were God's first temples.

2. All that tread
The globe are but a handful to the tribes
That slumber in its bosom.

3. Loveliest of lovely things are they
On earth that soonest pass away.

4. Innocent child and snow-white flower!
Well ye are paired in your opening hour.

5. When you can pipe that merry old strain,
Robert of Lincoln, come back again.

6. The maples redden in the sun;
In autumn gold the beeches stand.

7. These gay idlers, the butterflies,
Broke to-day from their winter shroud.

8. On woodlands ruddy with autumn
The amber sunshine lies.

To the Teacher. — A conversation exercise should follow or precede the writing of these extracts.

LESSON IV.

Supplementary Reading.

In these Language Exercises you have frequently been asked to read and to study poems, and then to express in your own words the ideas that you had gained from the reading and study. These poems are thought to be among the best productions of American poets.

Besides books of poems, there are many other books well worth your reading. No doubt you have read many that are excellent, and can remember much that you have read.

1. Make a list of the titles of books which you have read within six months.

2. Write a short account of the book with which you are most familiar.

To the Teacher. — Arrange the names of the pupils alphabetically in a blank-book, and under each name note the books and papers that have been read by the pupils recently. For this purpose, pupils may make a weekly report to the teacher. Thus, a careful watch can be kept over the pupils' reading, and opportunity will be given for valuable suggestions as to good books for future use.

At least one half hour each week should be set apart for conversation with pupils upon the books and papers they are reading.

LESSON V.
Neighborhood Study.
Topics for Conversation.

1. Vegetables, including trees; kinds and uses.
2. Wild flowers, names and description.
3. Business of the people; farming; different kinds of manufactures; trade or commerce.
4. Beautiful scenery; describe it. Tell in what its beauty consists.
5. Public buildings or other works of art, such as monuments, statues, etc.

To the Teacher. — Such lessons as the above may be made interesting and profitable, if the pupils are led to observe carefully, and to make orderly reports of what they have learned.

It may be necessary to divide such lessons as this into two or three, in order to give the pupils more time to investigate the different subjects.

LESSON VI.
Composition.

Write upon one or more of the topics given in the preceding lesson, giving a full and interesting account of what you have learned and how you learned it.

LESSON VII.
Review Exercise.

The following words are selected from certain lessons already learned. First tell from what root-word each is derived, and then use the root-word in a sentence.

broken	gone	frozen	blown
done	given	fallen	shaken
bitten	drawn	seen	spoken
eaten	flown	written	stolen
driven	forgotten	grown	taken

You will notice that the words all end in *n* or the sound of *n*. What can you tell about the use of such words? Can you name the five forms of which each word in the foregoing list is one?

LESSON VIII.

Historical Letter.

To the Teacher. — Read the story of the battle of Lexington to the children. Make it as graphic as possible, so that the pupils will form a mental picture of the route from Boston to Lexington which was followed by the British. Let them picture the farm-houses on the route, the country people leaving their work to watch the soldiers, — the men and older boys taking their guns and following through the woods and fields, — the scene on Lexington Common, — the destruction of the stores in Concord, — the retreat to Boston, — the Americans hiding behind walls, trees, and houses, and firing upon the British soldiers. Also read Bryant's stirring poem, "Seventy-Six," Holmes's "Lexington," and Longfellow's "Paul Revere." Then, with the pupils, prepare notes from which the letter may be written.

Suppose you were living near Lexington on the 19th of April, 1775, and saw all that has been described to you in the story of the battle of Lexington. Write a letter to your cousin living in England, and give an account of what you saw and heard on that memorable day.

LESSON IX.

Conversation Exercise.

1. Find out all that you can about *metals* from your own observation, from books, from your teacher, and from any other source possible.

2. Use the following notes and such others as you may wish to add:

What are metals? Different kinds. Where found? One of the most common. Some of its qualities. Some of the uses of this metal.

If this metal could not be obtained, what other metal might take its place? Why?

3. Write what you have learned, arranging your work in an orderly manner.

LESSON X.

Words often Mispronounced.

heroine	genuine	preventive
heroism	national	rational
docile	patriotic	lamentable
impious	patriotism	hospitable

Make careful preparation of the spelling, pronunciation, and meaning of the words in the foregoing list. Copy the words, separating them into syllables, and mark the vowel sounds. The following will indicate errors in pronunciation to be guarded against:

1. Sound the vowel in the first and in the third syllable of the first and second words of the foregoing list.

2. What sound has the vowel in each syllable of the third?

3. Pronounce the accented syllable of the fourth. Sound i in the second syllable.

4. Sound the i in the fifth word?

5. Sound the vowel in the first syllable of the sixth.

6. Sound the a in the seventh and eighth. Which syllable is accented in each?

7. How many syllables in the ninth?

8. Sound the a in the first syllable of the tenth.

9. Which syllable is accented in the eleventh? Sound the vowel in the accented syllable.

10. Sound the accented syllable in the twelfth?

11. Name the primitive words in the first, second, fourth, sixth, seventh, eighth, ninth, and eleventh.

12. Pronounce the primitive and then the derivative of each word called for in question eleven.

13. Define each word and use it in a sentence.

LESSON XI.
Composition.

To the Teacher.— Read with the children Bryant's beautiful poem, "Robert of Lincoln." See how much they can learn from the poem of the life, habits, and character of the bobolink. After the discussion of the poem, read Irving's sketch on the same subject. Then have a composition written, each pupil to introduce one or more extracts from the poem.

LESSON XII.
Uses of Words.
First *oral* and then *written*.

1. Tell the uses of the words and phrases between the vertical lines in the following selection:

"I can" | climbs | to the mountain-top, |
And | plows | the billowy | main; |
He | lifts | the hammer | in the shop, |
And | drives | the saw | and | plane. |

2. What two words are used as one name?

3. What word is used instead of a name?

4. What is the name for which it is used?

5. Select all the nouns and write them in the opposite number.

6. Add an apostrophe and the letter *s* to *mountain*, and use the word in that form in a sentence.

LESSON XIII.

Historical Letter.

To the Teacher.— Read to the pupils, from some good history, the story of the "Landing of the Pilgrims," and read Bryant's poem, "The Twenty-Second of December." Tell them about the "Mayflower," and some of the most noted persons who came in that vessel; also of their sufferings during the first winter. Finally, read with the pupils "The Courtship of Miles Standish."

At a subsequent lesson, require them to make notes of what they have learned about the Pilgrims.

1. Suppose yourself to have been one of the "Pilgrims," and that you were one of the soldiers who fought under the leadership of Miles Standish.

2. Write a letter to some friend in England, giving an account of your experiences.

LESSON XIV.

Telegrams.

The cost of sending a telegram depends upon the number of words in it. The words in the *heading, address,* and *signature,* are not counted as parts of the telegram.

In writing telegrams, be sure to express your ideas clearly and in the fewest words possible. Unimportant words are usually omitted.

The following despatch was recently received:

"Cars off track. None hurt. Shall be two hours late."

This means, "The cars are off the track, but no one is hurt. I shall be at home two hours later than I expected."

This telegram cost 25 cents. If it had been sent in the second form, the expense would have been much greater.

Write from the notes below, telegrams of not more than ten words each:

1. You want ten copies of Charles Dickens's "Pickwick Papers" forwarded from Harper & Brothers, New York, to your store in Boston.

218 LANGUAGE EXERCISES.

2. Engage a state-room on board a steamer that leaves Fall River for New York to-night.

3. You have unexpectedly met an old acquaintance, and have invited him to dine with you at home. Send a telegram to your mother informing her of the fact.

4. Telegraph to your brother, asking him to meet you. Name time and place.

5. You have just reached Liverpool, after a stormy voyage of ten days. Send by *cable* a telegram of fewer than five words, informing your friends of your safe arrival.

LESSON XV.

1. Write a connected account of the way in which you spent your last vacation.

2. Make and arrange your notes without help.

To the Teacher. — The object of this lesson is to find out whether the pupils have profited by their instruction in composition-writing.

LESSON XVI.

Oral Paraphrase or Conversation.

The following stanzas were taken from Bryant's poems:

1. Cool shades and dews are round my way,
    And silence of the early day;
        'Mid the dark rocks that watch his bed,
        Glitters the mighty Hudson, spread
    Unrippled, save by drops that fall
    From shrubs that fringe his mountain wall;
        And o'er the clear still water swells
        The music of the Sabbath bells.
            From " A Scene on the Banks of the Hudson."

2. The bluebird chants from the elm's long branches,
   A hymn to welcome the budding year.
   The south wind wanders from field to forest,
   And softly whispers, "The Spring is here."
   From "An Invitation to the Country."

3. The breath of spring-time at this twilight hour
   Comes through the gathering gloom,
   And bears the stolen sweets of many a flower
   Into my silent room.
   From "May Evening."

4. New are the leaves on the oaken spray,
   New the blades of the silky grass;
   Flowers that were buds but yesterday,
   Peep from the ground where'er I pass.
   From "The Old and the New."

5. Wild was the day; the wintry sea
   Moaned sadly on New England's strand,
   When first the thoughtful and the free,
   Our fathers, trod the desert land.
   From "The Twenty-Second of December."

To the Teacher.—See Lesson XVII., Chapter Nine.

LESSON XVII.

Advertisements.

To the Teacher.—Select from some newspaper half a dozen advertisements and write them on the blackboard. Call attention to the forms, and give such instruction as the pupil will need in the following lesson.

1. Write an advertisement for a situation as book-keeper in some large store. State your qualifications and give references.

2. Write such an answer to your advertisement as you would like to receive.

3. Advertise the loss of a watch, giving some particulars, and offering a reward.

4. Write an advertisement, stating that you have found a watch which the owner can have by proving property and paying charges.

LESSON XVIII.

Dictation and Conversation Exercise.

After writing the following proverbs, tell their meaning in your own words:

1. The sleep of a laboring man is sweet.
2. The borrower is servant to the lender.
3. Faithful are the wounds of a friend.
4. The wicked flee when no man pursueth.
5. Give me neither poverty nor riches.
6. Remember now thy Creator in the days of thy youth.
7. Drowsiness shall clothe a man with rags.
8. Wisdom is the principal thing, therefore get wisdom.
9. Be not righteous overmuch.
10. Cast thy bread upon the waters, for thou shalt find it after many days.
11. A word fitly spoken is like apples of gold in pictures of silver.
12. Look not thou upon the wine when it is red, ... at the last it biteth like a serpent, and stingeth like an adder.

To the Teacher. — If desirable, this lesson may be divided into two exercises.

LESSON XIX.

Review Exercise.

The following words have been selected from preceding lessons on "Verb-forms," and they are all taken from the fourth column of words in your tables:

sat	lay	took	went	flew
shook	gave	chose	wrote	came
rose	blew	wore	saw	drove
grew	began	threw	ate	did

1. Write from memory the first and the fifth form for each word.
2. Use each word in the columns, in an oral sentence, clearly indicating the time referred to.

LESSON XX.

Study and commit to memory the following poem, making it the basis of a conversation exercise:

THE GLADNESS OF NATURE.

1. Is this a time to be cloudy and sad,
   When our mother nature laughs around;
   When even the deep blue heavens look glad,
   And gladness breathes from the blossoming ground?

2. There are notes of joy from the hangbird and wren,
   And the gossip of swallows through all the sky;
   The ground-squirrel gaily chirps by his den,
   And the wilding bee hums merrily by.

3. The clouds are at play in the azure space,
   And their shadows at play on the bright green vale,
   And here they stretch to the frolic chase,
   And there they roll on the easy gale.

4. There's a dance of leaves in that aspen bower,
   There's a titter of winds in that beechen tree,
   There's a smile on the fruit, and a smile on the flower,
   And a laugh from the brook that runs to the sea.

5. And look at the broad-faced sun, how he smiles
   On the dewy earth that smiles in his ray,
   On the leaping waters and gay young isles,
   Ay, look, and he'll smile thy gloom away.
                              WILLIAM CULLEN BRYANT.

To the Teacher.—Read with the pupils any or all of the following poems. Conversation should of course be a part of each exercise: "Song of Marion's Men," "The Land of Dreams," "The Wind and the Brook," "Seventy-Six," "To the Fringed Gentian," "The Green Mountain Boys," The White-Footed Deer," "To a Mosquito," and "The Little People of the Snow." See page 223.

LANGUAGE EXERCISES. 223

Poems Used or Referred to in the Preceding Pages.

THESE may be found in the Complete Works of the authors, and in the smaller collections, many of which have been prepared especially for school use.

The teacher is strongly urged to make the reading of the various authors as broad and comprehensive as possible. The lessons in the book are only suggestive of a very extended line of language study, upon the same general plan, in connection with the reading and memorizing of the best productions of standard writers.

The poems of Bryant are published by D. Appleton & Company, 1, 3, and 5 Bond Street, New York.

The writings of the Cary Sisters, Holmes, Longfellow, Lowell, and Whittier are published by Houghton, Mifflin & Company, 4 Park Street, Boston, Mass.

The Household Editions of these various authors are published at about $1.50 each, postpaid. The smaller collections referred to can be obtained of the publishers named above, postage paid, at from 15 cents to 60 cents each. Among those of special service to teachers are:

MODERN CLASSICS.—Vol. 1.—LONGFELLOW: Evangeline; The Courtship of Miles Standish; Favorite Poems. Vol. 4.—WHITTIER: Snow-Bound; The Tent on the Beach; Favorite Poems. Vol. 5.—LOWELL: The Vision of Sir Launfal; Favorite Poems. Vol. 30.—HOLMES: Favorite Poems; My Hunt after the "Captain."

THE RIVERSIDE LITERATURE SERIES.—No. 1.—Longfellow's Evangeline. No. 4.—Whittier's Snow-Bound and Among the Hills. No. 5.—Whittier's Mabel Martin, Maud Muller, and Other Poems. No. 6.—Holmes's Grandmother's Story and Other Poems. No. 11.—Longfellow's The Children's Hour and Other Poems. Nos. 13, 14.—Longfellow's The Song of Hiawatha. No. 30.—Lowell's The Vision of Sir Launfal and Other Pieces. No. 33.—Longfellow's Tales of a Wayside Inn, Part I. No. 38.—Longfellow's The Building of the Ship and Other Poems.

BRYANT LEAFLETS for Homes, Libraries, and Schools.

HOLMES LEAFLETS, containing A Ballad of The Boston Tea Party, Lexington, The Comet, etc.

LONGFELLOW LEAFLETS, containing Paul Revere's Ride, The Building of the Ship, The Children's Hour, and Other Selections.

WHITTIER LEAFLETS, containing Barbara Frietchie, Mabel Martin, Maud Muller, The Three Bells, etc.

Teachers will do well to procure from the various publishers catalogues and lists of special issues of standard works for school use.

www.ingramcontent.com/pod-product-compliance
Lightning Source LLC
Chambersburg PA
CBHW021823230426
43669CB00008B/851